I GOT THIS OLD IN AN HOUR

An Anthology For Living At 24 Frames Per Second

I GOT THIS OLD IN AN HOUR

An Anthology For Living At 24 Frames Per Second

By Mike Hirsch

Katydid Publishing
Muncie, Indiana

I Got This Old In An Hour
An Anthology For Living At 24 Frames Per Second

By Mike Hirsch
As Published in In-Sync Publications

Copyright © 1997 by Katydid Publishing

Library of Congress Catalog Card Number
97-72245

ISBN 1-888349-03-4
Printed in the United States of America

Published by Katydid Publishing,
A Division of The Mug Joint., Inc.
P.O. Box 2247, Muncie, In 47307, USA
(765) 282-3159

Direct inquiries and/or orders to the above address.

All rights reserved. Except for use in a review, no portion of this book may be reproduced in any form without the express written permission of the publisher.

Neither the author nor the publisher assumes any responsibility for the use or misuse of information contained in this book.

FORWARD

My father talked a lot when I was little. He told me the way things were, the way things were going to be, and the way things were supposed to be. I stared at the wall.

"You've closed your ears and turned off your brain," he would say. I would stare at the wall. Who listened to their father? What did he know? I didn't need his lectures. The talking continued.

Since I've been away from home I've been amazed by how many times I hear his voice, his advise, in my head. Over and over again I hear his catch phrase—cover your butt, don't take any guff, and listen to the music. Every day his advise is put into play. What amazes me is how I heard every word he'd ever said.

Reading this collection might work the same way for you. You might finish an article and say, "Okay, so what?" Then one day, perhaps tomorrow, next week, next year, possibly even several years from now, you will get the message. Make movies.

Amber E. Hair

DEDICATION

It's too late for me to dedicate a book. My grandma and my Aunt Liz showed me God. My father taught me courage, stand up, and the value of a good left hook. My mother taught me about duty and fealty. My children taught me pain and joy. And my wife gave me first herself, and then the universe. Who would you thank?

I write this blurb every month for a variety of reasons. First, I want to cheer for all of you tough and bright enough to pursue this insanity in your own way. Second, I want you to be aware that the whole human story is an amazing and wonderful wellspring of material. I have never met a man or woman whose life wasn't worth a full length screen play. Most of us are invisible to God and history. We lead lives of desperate chance and folly punctuated by insight and love and fear and wonder. Living inside the skin that holds us up has a tendency to limit our realization of the thrill and horror and bliss of our own experience. Most of the things I write are universal in their nature but still seem foreign when we see them through another's eyes.

I try not to pontificate too much, but I'm aware that I am both color and status blind to the core of my being. I absolutely believe that we are only as safe and strong and powerful as our unity as human beings allows us to be. I think the enemy of us all is the hater and the bigot and the coward. History proves that building great fortifications against the dark possibilities of life is a waste of time. Great ruins with walls forty and fifty feet thick prove my point. We only get to keep what we share, and grow stronger with every new citizen we make. I believe this is the job of a man. Our life's work is worthless unless we are taking forward steps, and dragging others forward with us.

Mine is not the only viewpoint. We are surrounded by men with agendas so dark that most of us can't imagine such motivation. They come disguised as teachers and healers and religious leaders and political types and have great carriage and presence. They don't lie to you about what they believe, they simply make their odd sense of reality seem reasonable and proper.

For them, all is designed to protect the status they either enjoy or lust after, a near perfect mirror of reality. Unless you pay great attention, you are never, or seldom, aware that they are hiding their fear in what seems to be reason. Those who try to tell you that we are in danger of losing our souls or lives or ethics have only themselves to fear. The only way for us to fail is to stop caring for ourselves and our brothers. The best way to fight poverty and despair and violence is to make every man a citizen, with full franchise and portfolio.

In spite of what the prevailing attitude is, we will not make ourselves stronger by abandoning the impoverished or different or fearsome. For two hundred years we have been the hope of humanity. How can any of us, while sitting at the top of the heap, take it upon ourselves to doubt that our success as a people and a nation is the will of divine providence. The power hungry think we will abandon reason for security—show them. Make movies.

I Don't Run Except In My Dreams

The first great dragon in my life was my maternal grandfather. He was a hard man who fled Ireland in front of the law and never looked back. He arrived in time to become a trooper in a Michigan Militia Brigade that lost ninety percent of the kids who joined to fight the bloody rebels. He was in Reno's column when Custer made his great mistake at the Little Bighorn River and finally left the western army when Geronimo gave up the chase. He was still working his own place when he died in 1951. He was a hundred and five and had three kids under twenty years old. His wife was forty-two and seemed happy. They had been married for twenty-six years. The words "dirty old man" come to mind.

He had ridden with Sherman and Grant and shook hands with Lincoln. He was attaché to the young General Custer who aided at the surrender of Robert E. Lee, and held the old man's horse as Lee mounted to lead the rebels home. He buried wives and children and friends and enemies for over a century and taught me how to ride a horse. It is the first lesson I remember, and the most important.

In a world of wide, comfortable, western saddles, the monster made me use the same kind of butt pad the old horse cavalry used. It was very small and uncomfortable with no horn and a split running fore and aft to make it easy on the horse. A McClelland saddle was the barest kind of gear and designed with weight in mind. Kind of like a running shoe, very light but hard on the user.

Grandpa made me ride for the horse; my feet well forward, gripping tightly with my knees. My back had to stay ramrod straight because slouching made the load hard on the animal.

In the western heat and dust the discipline was hell on a kid under eight. One afternoon, on the way home from a particularly hard ride, I managed to get far enough ahead to relax and ride for a moment like a sack of potatoes. The monster knew boys well enough to know what I had in mind, and he made up enough distance to catch me looking like a lump on one of his horses. He didn't raise his voice; he didn't have to. He made me get off and walk the four miles to the house, leading the horse. He was right, and I never forgot the lesson.

It seems a simple way to make a profound point. In order to make the best use of the horse, I had to give up something. An easy lesson for a small boy—harder for grown men who sometimes forget that we have to give in order to get. Simple advice; keep your back straight and your feet well forward. What's easy on you is not usually good for the craft. Compromise is far easier than it should be. Sit up straight—make movies.

My grandmother was only fifteen and a child bride when she first saw the great statue we call Liberty. She was a Sephardic Jew. She was blond and fair with no hint of the darker Spanish blood that made such a mark on her older sisters and brothers. When the giant Russian madman who was to be my grandfather carried her off, everyone but her mother cried. My great grandmother was a tough old monster who abraded the rest of the family of scholars and merchants who felt so superior to him. Odd that time and a world gone mad would murder all of them. To the last soul they died in the camps and ghettos of Europe.

Forty odd years and a lifetime of privilege separate us. I can still feel and hear her in my memory, softly murmuring the prayer and lighting the Sabbath candles. I loved her. Fate had her mother eleven children of mixed talents and realities who made much of the miracle America allowed them. They were an unruly bunch and noisy in a manner strange to the gentile folk who were their neighbors. They faced a prejudice here little different from the kind most Jews faced everywhere, but America was their salvation. This is a memory of the death of her past and mine, and why I feel so strongly about how men must treat one another.

From the day she arrived in the new world she wrote to her cousins and sisters and brothers and aunts with the fealty her time demanded of good daughters. She said the prayers every day for those whose faces she could not recall. For fifty years she traded pictures and stories and prayers with a family she would never see again. The duty to God she had learned at the feet of her mother made the ancient rituals appealing and immeasurably strengthening to the sons and daughters she bore in her own time. The truth of the Old Book was as real to her as the daily newspaper. She knew God because she had talked to him every day of her life. She never questioned her place in space or time because Torah answers those questions for the faithful. She never faltered until the light vanished from the world she'd made in this land.

Americans didn't know about the death camps. The great mystery of that horror was thrust upon them in the blinking of an eye. All of them who were old enough to understand suddenly knew what "Jew" meant for much of the world. The letters unreturned and unread for four or five years had been carefully filed and stored by the murderers. The very moment she heard the truth she pulled the old shawl around her shoulders and began the prayers for the lost. More had died than still lived and how would the prayers ever cover all of those lovers and friends and strangers who were gone, forever? We still murder and pray. Make it stop. Make movies.

My wife's grandmother was married at sixteen. She weighed in at about ninety pounds, soaking wet, and in 1889 married a coal miner from Scotland who seemed to be made of iron. He wasn't very tall, but working the forge and shoeing the mules that moved the great loads of coal into the light gave him the arms and torso of a much larger man. He was a coronet player of some note and strikes a proud and handsome pose in the picture of the band organized by the miners in Crested Butte, the mining town they lived in when married. He had worked fourteen hour shifts in the mines from the morning of his tenth year and was married at twenty one. Grandma was a first generation American, second daughter, fifth child, of English-Irish immigrants who came to America as bond servants.

Grandma's mother served ten years in this country to pay back a three hundred dollar package that included sixteen dollars for steerage fare. She was twenty-eight when she married, and her husband was forty. She finally had twenty-one children, only three stillborn. She buried two husbands and died in 1941, the year my wife was born. She was over one hundred years old. She was an old woman before electric lights or automobiles or welfare or collective bargaining. If there was no work she had nothing. Until she was sixty she had never seen a doctor, or a hospital, or a store that was not owned by "The Company". Her people found no particular freedom in the payment of their bond-debt; she spent her life making citizens of her children. It was only slightly less difficult for them.

Grandma would live through labor wars and lock outs and

strikes and lousy health care and hard work and great pain to become a card carrying citizen of this country. She saw the end of company stores and Pinkerton agents and gun carrying bullies and police actions. She saw them pass from the front lines of the American labor movement. Like every part of the American experience, no matter what your name was or where you had become brothers in order to become citizens, this epic journey, from immigrant to citizen, is the most profound part of the American story. All of them—no matter where they had started—became part of the greatest political force in human history: The American Citizen.

We still have the power to make the world shake and tremble. We have to retrain the children and grandchildren of those early immigrants. We have to reinvent the unity that finally made our parents and grandparents free. I believe that the greatest purpose of you, the communicators, is to tell the old stories, again and again, until all of our children know the truth of our power when we are one. Fight about what you think the truth is, but do it where our children can learn from the fight. Make movies.

My Uncle Sticky died this month. He was the old man's youngest brother and a real outlaw. When Richard Dreyfuss played *The Tin Man* or when Robin Williams sold Cadillacs or when Robert De Niro drove a taxi cab or Marlon Brando played a gambler in a musical, they were all "doing Sticky". He wouldn't have made your mother proud (my own grandmother probably died sighing his name with her last breath) but you'd have loved him. He was a man with no compromise. He didn't drink, but it's the only vice I'm aware of that he didn't revel in. He was a gambler by trade and choice and natural selection and bullheaded obstinacy. He never held a legitimate job in is life. He was rakish—well dressed—immaculately groomed—as selfish as a child—and charitable to a fault. He'd give you the shirt off his back and then steal the pennies off a dead man's eyes. I loved him.

Sticky always drove a new Cadillac—Oldsmobile—Buick, fire-engine something color, as fast as it would go. He lived in the most expensive apartments money could buy, bought new furniture when he felt a color change coming on, demanded bloody-red rare meat three times a day and expected to sit at the best table. If he didn't want to talk to you he wouldn't answer the phone, and when you finally caught up with him, you got no apology. He was the greatest Pan player that ever lived and made a living beating the dogs. Four Vegas hotels sued him in five states trying to collect.

True story: Incredibly famous big time criminal lawyer—household word, Phi Beta Kappa, Summa Cum golden boy, first name basis with presidents, kings and Mafia dons. Enter

Sticky, shaken—disheveled—ushered quickly into lawyer's office. Gangsters are after him—carrying a bag of uncut diamonds stolen from gangsters—Sticky has to get out of town. "Please help me, famous lawyer, cynical all-wise defender of the innocent or guilty alike." Open bag—flash glittering hoard under the startled and greedy nose of intrepid lawyer—a hundred thousand dollars? Fifty thousand dollars? Gives Sticky five thousand dollars—throws diamonds in safe—doesn't touch them for six months. Takes them out of safe—sends them to world class jeweler—picks two biggest stones, "Make me cuff links". Jeweler calls—"are you sure?" "Yes", says lawyer. Now has pair of cuff links—left one has a "car", right one has a "fri"—part of the raised lettering on the bottom of the Carlson-Frink milk bottle Sticky broke up in an alley and sold to the lawyer for five thousand dollars.

The famous jeweler charged the famous lawyer six hundred bucks to make the cuff links, and the famous lawyer still wore them to court the last time I saw him—to remind himself how smart he really was. As for Sticky—spent the five thousand—never apologized to anybody—died of old age surrounded by people who loved him. (Almost. My sister lured his widow away from his side at the final moment for a cup of coffee that she really needed because—what could happen?) I'll miss him. Make movies.

I come from a jaded background. My father and uncles were generally less than easy to get along with. I know the reasons and have no inclination to expound them here. Suffice it to say that they had little potential to be citizens in the common sense, and so they followed a different drummer. The path they chose was a difficult one that compelled them to be very hard and aggressive with scant regard for propriety. In a nutshell, they were gangsters.

I know enough history to forgive them for whatever menace they appeared to be and know their characters well enough to know that they weren't cheap or petty in the things they did. When the old man died, over a thousand people showed up at his funeral on two days' notice. The tears shed were real, and the regard shown for the old dragon was impressive. I will likely not fare as well.

He had lived his life in conflict with a society that thrust him into a second class citizenship because of what he was, not who he was. At an early age he opted not to live the life that the power dictated for him. I have lived long enough to come to the conclusion that he was the best kind of American. I am convinced that if you are to succeed in this odd business, you will have to get out of the line most men are willing to stand in. We are "outlaws" in a very real sense. We either choose to be free of the shackles that the power wants to bind the communicators with, or we become the worst kind of cowards.

You young men and women have a larger problem than I had; you are less aware of your roots and family than I was. Perhaps your family is larger than mine was. You may have to speak for all of the powerless, while all I had to do was speak for myself. After all of the lives that went before me, I am no more safe from the monsters at the top of this heap than my father and uncles were. I have a power they didn't have. I can tell the stories of the powerless and disenfranchised with a strength that comes from knowing how like them I am. If you haven't ever questioned what position you fill, you may not care about who or what I am, but be assured that I care about you. I think that we can ensure that at some future day there will be no powerless.

If you don't care, get out of the way. If you have the power and are mortally afraid of we who would take our place with you, prepare for the worst. If you feel special because of the meaningless differences between people, you don't count. If you have spent your life falling in line with the status-quo, you are responsible for much of the pain that walks the world today. If you have the tools and gifts to make a mark for the ones who can't speak for themselves and you don't, damn you. If your story tells the truth—make movies.

If you were ten years old in 1945, there were a lot fewer things to lust after. Even guys from my generation have a hard time remembering when there was nothing here—no fast food, no plastic, no discount, no credit, no nothing. In our house we were still six years away from our first refrigerator and "made in Japan" meant dive bombers and machine gun bullets. No one had ever seen a tract house or an interstate highway or a credit card. It made some very normal things real important to you. This is about the best hamburger in the world.

Denver was the big city (that translates as cow town with a May Company store and a downtown shopping area six blocks long on both sides of the street—no shopping centers or discount stores for another fifteen years.) The Brown Palace Hotel was one of the five most famous hotels in the world, and the Shirley-Savoy across the street, had just been finished. From this megalopolis to the ranch was a two hundred and fifty mile drive down a mostly two lane dirt road, and backwards in time a hundred years; no running water, no electricity, no inside plumbing, closest supplies the mine company store in Trinidad fifty miles away. You cooked with wood, and if it was meat, you killed it yourself. The greatest hamburger in the world was back up the road towards Denver one hundred and eighty miles.

The earliest thing I remember reading was a sign that said "WORLD'S GREATEST HAMBURGER". It was in Colorado Springs half way through town on the right hand side as you went south. Colorado Springs was a class place for rich people. The road through town was divided, one side going south—one side going north—big statue of a guy on a horse right in the middle downtown. (I don't know who he was, but there was a plaque on the bottom that said "Keep Right". Until I die I'll remember him as "General Keep Right".) You didn't pass two restaurants in that two hundred fifty miles. In my whole life until that time there were no restaurants, but there was that sign, "WORLD'S GREATEST HAMBURGER". I swear to you I've never wanted anything more—not money, not car, not woman, not fame, not nothin'—I just wanted a taste of the world's greatest hamburger.

I never got it. I guess to the old man a kid wanting to stop more than a hundred miles from the ranch to eat a hamburger must have sounded like the most pointless thing in the whole wide world. I know he never stopped. I think he knew how bad I wanted it, and the fifteen or twenty cents the world's greatest hamburger would have cost couldn't have been a deterrent. But sometimes, for reasons none of us understand, we resist the easiest ways to make the people we love happy. I've probably done it to my own kids, and I don't know why.

I think if the old man were alive and could do it over, he'd probably stop so we could share the world's greatest hamburger. I wish we could. Take your own kids out and buy a hamburger for me. Make movies.

Most of the time when some weird old guy tells a story about the talents he displayed as a youth, it's reasonable to smile politely, "uh huh" at the proper intervals, and ignore every word he says. In my experience listening is a total waste of time. Make an exception this time. I'm going to tell you a story about my amazing talents and my subsequent misuse and abuse of them. It won't take long because these things usually only run five hundred words or so.

I was a normal looking kid. My talent had nothing to do with matinee idol good looks or Atlas-like physique, nor did I have extraordinary athletic prowess. Very simply, I had the most beautiful singing voice you've ever heard. In the nineties everybody in the world is a singer (assuming that rap is music and doesn't really suck). But the truth is, God gave me a one in a trillion voice. When I sang, rodeo crowds stopped what they were doing to listen. You may think this is an exaggeration, and I'll remind you again, for the millionth time, that I never exaggerate. I had the most beautiful voice in the world.

I loved singing—I loved sad songs and glad songs and mad songs and silly songs and swing and rock and opera and rhythm-and-blues and country-and-western and especially the cantor songs in the synagogue. I think all human song is a glory to God, but the cantor was special.

The sad thing about my life is that I was the first generation of Americans raised and motivated to the foolhardy standard that the success or failure of a thing is somehow bound to its financial worth—the most preposterous theory in the history of the world. Some things are worth doing just because of what they are.

I loved singing so much that I did it for nothing, in restaurants—in supermarkets—in the car—everywhere. And I was lucky enough to find people who loved to sing with me. And I really think that, like old Pete Seger or Woody Guthrie or one of those strange old men, I should have just gone from pillar to post with the people I love singing everybody's songs.

I didn't. Finally the saddest thing in my life is that I let somebody convince me that doing something for the pure unbridled joy of it—for the applause and the bow—was imprudent. It made me afraid that the good feeling wasn't enough because I couldn't enter it on a ledger sheet. And so instead of being a joyful grasshopper kind of human being, singing boundless song to the glory of man and God, I became a "producer"—glib and slick and cynical and smart and moneyed and cold and cheerless and easily forgotten except by the people who believe that money is the bottom line.

I don't leap tall buildings at a single bound anymore. I don't run except in my dreams, and all of the sins I regret are of omission not commission. Make love—make music—make movies.

I was twelve years old the first time someone expected me to act like a man. I didn't know they expected it. I doubt they knew. I was only marginally successful. At the same time I learned to work twelve hours a day and not cry about it, I blew up a feed and grain store. I remember I really got no more abuse for blowing up the grain store than I got pats on the back for learning to be a man. The truth is the people who love us expect both things from us—good and bad.

In 1945 two cowboys stepped out in the street in front of a saloon in Jackson Hole, Wyoming, and became the last two men to fast draw one of them to death in the time-honored tradition of the Old West. I only include this information to place Wyoming in time and space for you. In Wyoming men still worked for a hundred dollars a month and food. For reasons that are still too painful to put down here I found myself separated from home and hearth on a working cattle ranch in Lander, Wyoming. The next youngest hand was forty years old and, suffice it to say, there wasn't much "boy" in any of these cowboys.

I'd never been a man before but had no time to agonize about it. I worked without crying because there was nobody to cry to. I also learned to roll my own, keep myself clean, and the difference between stand up and shut up. I got honest lumps—some I earned—some I didn't; but nobody abused me. The lesson was simple: In real life we do real things.

Being the youngest and the newest I got some terrible jobs. The one I hated most was going to the grain and feed and filling hundred pound gunny sacks full of wheat germ and oats and cracked corn to mix winter feed for horses and milk cows. When it's at least a hundred degrees and the air doesn't move, the dust and dirt of the job are horrendous. One afternoon, after four or five days of this job, I ducked back out of sight and lit a cigarette to satisfy the first of my adult vices. When the match flared, so did the air, and ten seconds later I was standing in a brand new field where the grain and feed had been, naked as a jaybird, bald as an egg, and black as the ace of spades. (A little wheat dust in the air makes a hell of a bomb.) I didn't hear anything but a ringing noise and coarse laughter for a month. And I imagine if any of those old hands are still alive, I'm one of their favorite stories.

There were no law suits, no insurance adjusters, very little screaming and yelling. Ten cow hands and four times as many neighbors spent one long weekend rebuilding the grain and feed and laughing at a kid who was learning "man". At the end of the summer when the hands lined up to get paid, I got my five times one hundred dollars in fresh silver coin the boss got in Reno. In real life, people take care of one another—and get paid what they earn. Make movies.

During the summer between my fourteenth and fifteenth birthdays, my buddy George led me astray—ruined my career as a rodeo cowboy—introduced me to the wonders of women—and made my father, the cowboy, look like a jerk to the preacher. At fourteen I was kind of a porky kid (harbinger of the porky adult I became). George was a man; rippling muscles, confidence, courage, all in all the kind of boy all men wanted for their son. He was also a rat. I was a mystery to my father. He struggled manfully not to compare me to George, but he couldn't help noting that, while George had all of the wonder traits, I was mostly a product of the goofy gene.

The cowboy was paying George and me to break a dozen horses he'd bought at a government auction. (George knew how to break horses—I was there so George's manliness would rub off on me. Some of it did.) For about two weeks we diligently ran horses around a corral, hooted and hollered, and did enough cowboy stuff to fire the dream in my heart of becoming a great saddle bronc rider and champion. And then entered the Cherry sisters. The name is not poetic license; it is the name bestowed upon the two nubile, glorious creatures who lured George and me out of the corral and into the barn for the next ninety days. I will not bore you with an accurate description of what went on in the barn. Suffice it to say, it was wonderful. I'm sure George intended that this insanity only last a couple of days. He must have been more responsible than I. I never wanted it to end. I totally forgot about horses, rodeos, my father the cowboy—until suddenly on a Friday the old man asked me in passing how we were coming with his horses. I did the only responsible thing; I lied.

On the following Saturday while George and I, contrite and fired anew to finish our job, were letting the horses into the corral for the first time in three months, the old man arrived leading the preacher and his two chubby daughters. It slowly dawned on us that he was selling the preacher one of these freshly gentled horses for his daughters. We managed to subdue one, and with George hanging onto its tail and I, firmly holding its head with my teeth clamped onto its ear, prayed for divine intervention while the old man set the preacher's oldest chubby daughter on the horse. It quivered in shock, humped its back, and when the old man told George and me to let go and step back, it did a funny stuttering kind of a crow hop and exploded into that glorious move that rodeo cowboys call sunfishing, a beautiful pirouette in the air followed by a rigid bang-bang-bang on the ground, that launched the preacher's daughter over a fence into the muck, the old man into disgrace, and me into adolescent hell.

I won't describe the next year of my life. I think the old man forgave me before he died. We changed churches. And everything else I've done the rest of my life has been, somehow, easy. Make movies.

M y father wanted to be a cowboy. It's funny how that fact flavors everything I do in my life. I never wanted to be a cowboy. Most kids in my era grew up watching the great movie cowboys do wonderful things with six gun, horse, rope, guitar, and girl. But I shoveled feed over a stock fence when it was twenty below and the wind was blowing forty miles an hour. I never felt like singing when I was so cold, hot, dirty, frightened, hungry, sick, tired. I just felt like being something else. I was seventeen and riding with George (remember George?) in a thirty ton chain drive White truck stacked thirteen feet high, nine feet wide and forty five feet long with high class South Park hay the last time I ever did cowboy stuff.

It was terribly cold and the wind was blowing a ground blizzard. That's one of those western monsters you don't believe till you see them; no new snow but the wind blows the old snow—hard—eight feet high for a thousand miles. We broke a boom and dumped half a load of hay. It took both of us five hours to reload, and by the time we were done I was crying like a child. I have never cared to cowboy since. I went home, joined the Navy, and spent the next twenty years of my life somewhere else.

You'll notice that there's nothing extraordinary in this little tale if you're from the West. Stupid horses, hundred degree heat or twenty below zero cold, no water or flood. These are the things Westerners understand. Like Easterners understand delis, subways, traffic jams, muggings, and ethnic crazies. Different strokes for different folks. However, there is one difference. When the wind blows and a range cow feels like moving, he puts his nose into the wind, lowers his head, and walks. You don't turn him; you don't dissuade him; you don't stop him. When the wind blows and a horse feels like moving, he turns his back to the wind and walks. You don't turn him; you don't dissuade him; you don't stop him. That's everything there is to know about being a cowboy.

In the great screen play of Life I'm not sure which character I am. I might be the worthless son who abandons the family ranch and runs away to live with jaded show folks and do weird stuff till he gets his comeuppance. Or I might be the sensitive, talented, misunderstood son of earthy parentage who must go forth to find himself. If I was in a movie it would be lots clearer—my relationships with my father and cowboys and the rest of the world—but this is not a movie. I can't write bad scenes out of my past, and I can't write good scenes into my future. Neither can you. We, all of us, have to make do as best we can. (I hate that line.) That means we had best not drive ourselves too crazy over the mistakes we've made. By the same token, we had best not be too quick to take a great big bow when we luck into a happy ending. You've got to work hard—just don't work too serious. Have a good time. Make movies.

I n 1958 I saw a flying saucer. It was the strangest thing I'd ever seen. I have very little proof that I really saw the thing—but it made a big impact on me. I was standing the first mid-watch of my then fresh Navy days, and had only just begun to shake off the seasickness that I knew was going to kill me. The ship was an ancient, staggering hulk from WWII and had a round bottom that made us roll and pitch like a bad carnival ride. My watch was on the starboard (right) side of the ship's flying bridge, and I was dressed up like all the cool guys I'd seen in the movies.

I was wearing the greatest foul weather gear ever invented to stave off the cold and wet, had on the huge helmet that all of us official Navy watch guys wore to cover our heads, and the "sound powered phones" that we used to say important watch stuff to the rest of the guys running the ship. I was feeling very cool and squared away (a Navy phrase for correct in every fashion) and was light years away from the drudgery such watches would finally become. My mind's eye made me the match for John Wayne or Tyrone Power or Robert Taylor or any of the heroes who had sailed through the deadly waters of the South Pacific in a million great movies. I was not aware that in a few minutes I would flip my wig and report the appearance of the UFO that scared the hell out of me.

I had settled down to the task at hand and was all aglow with the pure "Navy" of it all, and for about an hour I never saw a thing but myself and the wonder of me on this ship on this ocean. Nothing in my past had prepared me to finally be where all of the matinee heroes of my childhood had been so many times. I was getting the walk and the cool lounging posture against the ship's rail down pat, and wishing all the guys at home could see me, when a flash of light caught my eye and changed my whole world—forever.

The amazing object leaped from the horizon to the top of the sky in the barest blink of an eye. It darted hither and yon with no regard for any of the natural laws of physics that Mr. Zinke had pounded into my head in eleventh grade science. I was aghast and beside myself at the same time, and all of my cool vanished in the twinkling of an eye. I began to scream bloody murder into my "sound powered phones" and was adamant that we were being at least pursued and probably about to be attacked by the UFO. The hatch to the bridge opened with a clang and most of the watch tumbled through it to witness either the UFO or my continued breakdown. At that moment I suddenly realized that I was watching the North Star—steady and secure where it always is in the night sky—and all of the movement was the ship's movement under me. I was the same goofy kid. Make movies.

My grandfather did not want to be a cowboy. He wanted to be an American. He was six feet four inches tall, had a magnificent dueling scar, and a half dozen bullet holes (all in the front) that he never explained. Coming to this country from somewhere in middle Europe in 1903 must have been horrendous, especially when he started, running, and never really believed that he'd escape. Somewhere on the trip he found my grandmother. When they arrived, she was fifteen years old, weighed eighty-five pounds and was carrying my Uncle Joe on her hip. She kept Grandpa out of America.

Grandma had never seen a black man before. When the ship arrived in New York City, they were met by a "cousin" who had sponsored them (probably a labor broker—big deal at the turn of the century). She asked the "cousin" what was wrong with those men whose skins were so dark. He told her that after you'd lived in America for a couple of years your skin turned black like that. She refused to get off the ship. So my father, the cowboy, was born in Canada. It took Grandpa another eleven years to get here.

It's a long way from my grandma and grandpa to me, the marcher—demonstrator—freedom rider—liberal—who has become American enough to see color as no obstacle to citizenry. By the time I was as old as my grandfather was when he got here he was gone but had replaced himself with a dozen Americans. Now I'm getting old, and I look around me and see a generation of children who don't realize that "American" is heart and soul and mind and dedication to a human dream undreamt in any other country. I learned about that American watching movies. Virtue is its own reward—the good guys always win—Americans are always the good guys.

Fighting humbug wars and launching space ships doesn't make us winners. As long as fifteen million Americans live in dire poverty we've got other fish to fry. Don't expect "doing the right thing" to be automatic. You communicators are the ones who set the standards that make adult Americans of little children; red, white, black, yellow, brown Americans. Spending a hundred million dollars squashing make believe mechanical boogie men doesn't seem as important as teaching my new grandchildren that Americans are the good guys, not because of airplanes and bombs and machine guns and fiery death, but rather because we have a sense of justice and fair play that makes it impossible for us to bully or take advantage of little guys. My grandfather didn't become a Mafioso; none of his children were divorced, imprisoned, or part of a major bank scandal. There are more Americans like Grandpa than Don Corleone.

Tell the truth—tell it happily—joyfully—lovingly—in red, white, black, yellow, brown. Make movies.

My father wanted to be a cowboy—big deal says you. Everybody's father wanted to be a cowboy. That might be true, but my father became one. He wasn't very good at it. He was also a tavern keeper. He was very good at that. It's funny, but he hated being a tavern keeper. He loved cowboying. It took every penny he could earn tavern owning to pay for his lousy cowboying.

What has this got to do, you might ask, with making a movie? Maybe nothing or maybe everything. Most people aren't unlucky enough to become their life's desire. Perhaps some people are better off not being cowboys. My mother and brothers and sisters and I would have been happier if the old man had stayed a tavern owner all of the time and only dreamed of cowboying. But I know that he was happiest doing dusty, disgusting, cowboy stuff in the wind and the rain and the heat of eastern Colorado. When he died, the trunk of his Buick held two old saddles, about half of a fifty pound sack of grain, three plastic washtubs, assorted curry combs and bridles and halters and such—and no tavern owner stuff. If I live to be a hundred I'll never forget that horsey, grainy, leathery smell when I opened the trunk of his car. I don't ever remember any tavern owner smell on him.

Making movies is a lot like cowboying. In order to persist you have to be unreasonable and impractical and maybe not too smart—just devoted to a dream and what you want to be. This missive in applause of cowboys and movie makers—long may you wave.

We Only Pass This Way Once

I think we've made a cult out of motivation. When Norman Vincent Peale wrote about *The Power of Positive Thinking*, he never intended to replace prayer with less. In 1960 when I was a baby just starting to be a man, the great motivators were beginning to flower. Peale, Ziegler, Nightingale, and the others were just beginning to explain the end results of a lifetime's study in why people didn't do what they could do. No matter what words they used, no matter how adept they were at saying it, it finally all boils down to the same thing—anything the average person has done more than once has become boring to him. Even if it earns our living, insures our future, protects our families, or makes us wealthy, we have to force ourselves to do it. And what's more important, we almost always refuse to do more than the minimum.

The motivators set out specialty collections of words designed to lift an educated, talented, knowledgeable human being equipped with all of the tools necessary to do the job he had to do, functioning inside the job he had to do, and make him do it. The words displayed the same old stuff in a different light every single morning, and it was motivating.

It's the nineties now, and the power of positive thinking is on the tip of everyone's tongue. We trot out the concept like we're warding off evil spells. The one thing all the great motivators stressed was that you had to first be well prepared and have all of those other assets before the motivation would make any difference. All of the skills and talents and knowledge plus the motivation formed a new machine that needed a real high class fuel to make it run—hard ass work.

We try desperately to solve all of our problems with positive thinking. Major size truth: If a thirteen year old uneducated inner city girl, pregnant with her second baby, insists everything is going to be all right, it will not make it so. She is—and is living—a disaster. Statistically she will not survive and bloom. She is doomed to live a calamity. Most of us are living the same kind of calamity as easily forecasted as prevented. We all know where our failure lies. If you divide a paper into two sides and list on one side all of the reasons you will fail and on the other all the reasons you might succeed, and do it honestly, the reasons for your failure are on that paper.

We should all make up this kind of list once a month and address the parts we can fix immediately. We'll be destroyed by the things we can't fix. If you understand and believe that, you'll fix things you didn't know you could. Make movies.

I like talking about hunting, fishing, skiing, boating, tennis, volleyball, jogging, working out. I hate hunting, fishing, skiing, boating, tennis, volleyball, jogging, working out. People who profess to enjoy all the above make me very uncomfortable because I lack the courage to tell them I hate all that stuff. A real successful camping trip for me implies that I be picked up at the airport in a 600-SE and deposited at my cabana at Kahuku Point, then continuously brought mint juleps and assorted red rare meat. I think I was always this way. Anybody who grew up where there is no green after the first of June and the dust is ankle deep at a hundred degrees unless it's mud, develops no fondness for walking, running, or jogging. The truth of the matter is that I come from real poor people. Most of them worked themselves to death. The dream was to get to the point where you could kick back. I guess I'm really lucky; I've never done anything my whole life but kick back.

This is really not about me. It's about the riots in Los Angeles. I'm old enough so that riots are not a new thing. I've seen them before all over the world. They're always about the same thing. No, I don't mean Rodney. That poor soul has already had a thousand times more attention than he ever deserved. The same is probably true of Chief Gates, the Mayor, Dan Quayle, Jesse Jackson and the rest of the cast of thousands that made this another really ludicrous public event. The riot was about people who don't have anything and, literally, have no hope of changing that fact. I think I've said this before; in the whole world ours is the only country where the quality of life is a question—everywhere else the question is whether you live or die.

American rioters are not motivated by the same kind of desperation that motivates people who are starving to death. Really hungry people in America are a monstrous exception not the rule. This riot was caused because people of all colors and creeds are doomed to raise their children in the middle of a trash heap, while the supposed-to-be community leaders spend more money saving dogs and cats and spotted owls than they'll spend on Head Start, Helping Hand, and day care programs.

When I started, seventy-five percent of our population was middle class or better. The average guy could still see himself in an elevated position if he worked hard enough. It doesn't appear as if the "average" believes that any more.

I like rare roast beef and soft recliners and girls that smell like warm showers, and I've never held a job in my life. In a land where more and more people are leading desperate and hopeless existences, I've been the proverbial grasshopper. I didn't come from big time famous parents; I've never had any money or education or bright future or faded past. I've just had wonderful luck, and I feel terrible because I don't know how to help one single soul who lived through that riot. If you do, tell somebody. Make movies.

There's one really good thing about being a poor boy—you're so easily satisfied. All it takes to make a real poor boy happy is money. He doesn't need security, he doesn't even believe in security. He doesn't need education, future, the acclaim of his peers. He doesn't need anything—just money. And unlike most rich guys, it doesn't take very much of that to make him happy. Kind of a sad truth about myself—that I'm as rich with a hundred dollar bill as I know how to be. My slice of the American Pie is really different from the slice a well-to-do citizen has. I think in ten thousand years of me, the largest estate went in your pocket or you rode it or you ate it or you had a party and drank it. I don't think fifty of me ever saved enough of anything in a lifetime to leave it to anybody. Most of us died doing something—building something—stealing something—chasing money. We settled America and Australia and Africa and, if you rich guys will leave us alone, we'll go to the stars.

I keep hearing about family values and certain high-brow politicians keep implying that they have the keys to the kingdom, that they are somehow blessed by the gods, and their portfolios are proof of it. Most poor boys learn one thing at a very tender age—old stuff that's not used much becomes garbage. That includes traditions that keep your ass in a chair, paralyze your mind with fear of the unknown, and alienate you from the guys that are building something. Old ideas are garbage, old prejudices are garbage, most old traditions are garbage, and most old money is garbage.

History proves one thing—that defending yourself is impossible. The landscape of every nation on earth is dotted with great fortifications—walls forty feet high and twenty feet thick—that were built by rich guys trying to save themselves and preserve family values. They were finally surrounded by people who didn't want or need anything except money—and the walls came tumbling down.

The only defense is a magnificent, preposterous, ridiculous, undisciplined, mindless offense. You feed poor people because you've got food. You house poor people because you've got space. You educate children because you know something you want somebody else to know. And if you measure the cost of it, you don't do anything. The real truth is the only way to get to the stars is to teach all those poor people how to get there, because you rich guys are going to sit on your asses and die trying to save something.

If you could eat anything you wanted any time you wanted, I'll bet you crispy ham fat wouldn't taste all that good. And in a world where twenty million children are going to starve to death this year, I don't want to hear one more word about cholesterol. A third of the human beings on the face of this earth sit in the dirt and boil gruel in a clay pot over sticks and twigs in a waddle hut. They measure their wealth and status with rings on their fingers and bells on their toes. So much for family values. Make movies.

I lived through the end of the world. In stories and films of the last moments there is much fire and smoke and noise and yelling. None of these things happened. The first sign of the end was a small, ugly collection of tract homes built out of cinder blocks and easily financed by something called FHA. If you were a veteran you could buy one of them without having any money. The ugly little shacks were soon everywhere.

That idea wasn't new, but for the first time in history all of the bankers in the world had lost their minds at the same time. This was the second sign of the end. These two things set off a wild era of falling ideals and declining values that had to pass for the fire and smoke and yelling that the movies use to show the end. The great myth was abound that somehow anyone could get anything he ever wanted without dedication or talent or skill or too much work. We invented a guy named "Tail Gunner" Joseph McCarthy, who invented communists and Russians and police actions and foreign aid and McDonalds.

Within thirty years of the end of the world, the Japanese managed to invent a 1950 Mercury and convince the public that it was a wonderful and new thing. The high priests trotted out K-Mart and Madonna and Rock 'N' Roll. It was hard to find any smoke or fire through all of the strange, boring stuff that made everyone lose twenty points of IQ. When the end finally came it was faithfully duplicated by Lucas with great morph effects and generated about thirty million dollars during its first five weeks at the theaters. Some guy with a furniture store in Altamont Springs is financing a sequel this summer. It will star Wayne and Garth.

While all of these strange and wonderful things were happening, educators were learning to not teach anything that required effort or grit or talent. They learned to graduate anyone. Since only the top twenty percent have the foggiest chance of surviving the real work involved in most intellectual pursuits, they avoided demanding anything that required talent or drive or genius. They learned to teach everything to the lowest common denominator. They taught nothing to everyone and developed real democracy. Everybody was stupid at the same time.

The world comes to an end for everyone sooner or later. All of the crying and teeth grinding and hand wringing and moaning won't stop it. We have wandered and stumbled and pushed our way around the world for a half million years or so, and the truth is, we'll probably keep stumbling for a lot longer. If any part of my ending is true, it's that everything new finishes something old. The new kids will do just fine. Of course, fifty years from now one of them will write about the end of the world. Don't worry—make movies.

Tomorrow is the first day of June and my grandson just got out of school for the summer. He will likely spend more time than he wants with me this year because his mom and dad are both working full time. He is thirteen, but we don't like the idea of leaving him to his own devices for too long. He's a good kid, but small towns are no better than big ones for latch key kids. It reminded me of another difference between now and then.

When I was his age I'd have already been out of school for six weeks. The truth of cattle ranches and farms is that you have to make hay while the sun shines. Spring roundup was a big deal. It was the first time you got to tally the losses of the winter and make some kind of plan to survive another year. The first full time expedition to the far corners of the ranch was a revelation; miles of fence taken out by spring run off or lightening, dead cows marked by their sad scattered bones and torn shriveling hides. You counted and hoped and planned and got over the ache that the first hard days planted deep in you. Even a kid got beat up by the first spring work.

I have a hard time believing that the work had any quality of sweatshop to it. We started learning the game when we were eight or nine, and by the time we were big enough to do the job, we knew what the work was. It seems a little irresponsible to me that a society with as many problems as ours seems to have compounds them by limiting how much our kids can learn about work and the value of it. We have passed laws that limit any entry into the job force to kids who are at least sixteen unless daddy owns the joint. I hear a lot of crap from people about cutting lawns and cleaning out garages, but it seems ridiculous to me to teach a kid that work is only drudgery. Hell, no matter how hard it was for me when I was learning, I had the fact of cowboy to sustain me.

When you get right down to it, I was probably pretty worthless when I started working hard. I was lucky enough to be surrounded by guys who understood that being a man means that you pass on what you know and what you are. They worked me and paid me and abused me until I was equal to the process of making a living. We should get back to that basic attitude. I have no way of knowing how hard it is to sell crack, but if I had way too much time on my hands and no hope, I'd probably learn.

If the law makes it impossible for a kid to learn about living, the law is probably no good. We need more room to teach the new ones how wonderful it is when you can make your own way. This is not about the poor or the hard pressed, it's about us and our kids. Make room—make movies.

Charlton Heston really ticked me off. So did Dennis Miller. I love Charlton Heston. When I think of God, he looks like Charlton Heston, and *Omega Man* is one of my ten top all time movies. Dennis Miller is capable of wonderful angst. Sometimes his rantings are sublime. This Friday last on the season's premier of his show, Charlton Heston was his guest. Miller started with a wonderful diatribe (if he more often than before appears to be forcing it, it's probably because it's hard to maintain real outrage about everything). For the most part it was about the senselessness of people shooting one another, willy-nilly, with guns that cost a nickel and can be had at a local swap meet. If he went over the top, so what? This subject appears to be one of those cases of the irresistible force meeting the immovable object.

I have to make a confession here. I personally have owned ten thousand guns starting with a J.C. Higgins single shot .22 the old man gave me when I was six. While I believe it's important that we keep the right to own and bear arms, I believe also that we must find a way to disarm violent children. I don't have an answer. History will afford one.

After introducing Mr. Heston (we, all of us, understood from the beginning that Mr. Heston was there because he is one of the great conservative dragons on our planet and could be counted on to be pro-gun. Some anti-gun people pretend his full name is Charlton "NRA" Heston), Mr. Miller asked a question that rambled for eleven minutes and did service to the best congressional committee question of all time. The point of the question was how could Charlton Heston really believe that guns were a good thing. Amidst considerable chuckling and hail-fellow-well-met-man-ship Mr. Heston replied with an answer that bordered on the ridiculous.

His opening gambit was to remind us all about the great quivering and quaking in East L.A. He then allowed as how a number of his liberal friends called him on the telephone wanting to borrow guns to defend their life and liberty. Naturally, since they were idiots (being liberal) who had never touched a fire arm before, he refused as they probably deserved whatever fate afforded them. I'm a liberal who can shoot your eyes out at a thousand yards, and some of the most conservative human beings I know are horrified at the idea of handling a gun. This is about labels.

I'm horrified by abortion—I have a wife and three daughters who have every right to make their own choices. I absolutely believe we have an obligation to care for the weak and poor and wounded—I also believe that real welfare reform is a necessity. I believe that sacrificing humanity on an alter of bombs is obscene—and I believe in a strong American military. I guess I'm a liberative or conservatal, and the world is more shades of gray than black and white. If you have an axe to grind, grind it; but remember that the liberal on the other side of the line you draw may be your own wife and three daughters. Make movies.

My youngest daughter and her husband just bought a small house on the west side of Indianapolis. It's their first real home in terms that mean something to average folks like his mom and dad. They "own it". If they want to tear down a wall, they can. They don't have to deal with a landlord anymore, and they are finally getting something besides rent receipts. The mark of citizen rests more firmly on their shoulders, and they have gained a stature that marks them as responsible and more capable than they were before. They are indebted for about thirty-five years or so, and will enrich the lender by double or triple the loaned amount. In a small sense, I feel wistfully disassociated from this happening as I have never had the slightest interest in buying a house. In fact, I have always been horrified at the prospect of living in any one place too long. Managing to finally pay off a loan on an old building has never had any particular charm for me.

This is not a new attitude on my part. From the time I was a small child I always had a great yearning to see what was over the next hill. I have lived the most independent life it's possible to live in our century, and part of that freedom was finding a wife and partner who had as much wanderlust as I did. We have owned million dollar carnival rides and led dozens of employees from pillar to post, but we have never owned a house. I think my mother-in-law went to her grave hating my guts because I am this way, and my family own great tracts of America in all corners of our country; but if it doesn't have wheels I don't like living in it.

My kids are nothing like me so I am willing to accept the fact that mine is the aberrant behavior, and the weakness seems to have lasted only one generation—mine. I have always marched to a different drummer and have long since lost any sense of longing to be more acceptable or normal, but I think the world is too wonderful and marvelous a place to see from one stoop. I know New York state in the fall and the high Rockies in the spring. I can close my eyes and breathe memories of purple and red desert skies or driving Louisiana rain. I have walked it and ridden through it and made love and war in most of the adjacent forty eight, and pretty much all of the world I could reach from where I started. I have given up a substantial part of the citizen's protection and comfort by living the way I have, but at this late date it was worth every discomfort.

I am not advocating that you jump right out and go on the road. The fact is that the peril may be so great now that most of you would have to pay too great a price. What I am asking is that you all understand how expensive some of civilization's trappings are. We were meant to wander and explore the great world around us, and closing the door on the adventure is the greatest price any of you will every pay. Don't give in. Make movies.

In an ugly little town in Colorado in 1914, my mother-in-law crawled down a blood-filled ditch escaping the machine gun bullets being fired at her by the duly appointed law. The governor of the state, in collusion with the coal mine owners, had hired gun slinging thugs from all over the country to put an end to a strike. The "marshals" were loaded into an armored car, along with fifty caliber machine guns and booze, and while they rode slowly through the tent town where the striking miners lived, they murdered the powerless.

I come from the throw-away people who died in America's mines and on her railroads and in her slaughter houses. My people fled something far worse to come here and raise children who became citizens of this place. That citizenship was paid for with the blood shed in the ugly little town, and the mines, and the slaughter houses. I am horrified that it has been so easy for me and my kind to forget how much it cost us. It still costs the newest among us a great deal to buy a future for their children.

Two things happened this year that cause me sadness on one hand and anger on the other. In Waco, the duly appointed law murdered women and children as defenseless as those in that ugly little town in Colorado. I don't care what flight of fancy launched an official government agency to decide that machine guns and tanks were a reasonable method of evicting a starry-eyed collection of religious coo-coos from their own brand of tent town, but it makes me angry that they were burned alive in my name.

The sadness was caused by the passing of Caesar Chavez

from the arena. He was the first of the "prefix" labor leaders. We have drifted so far from that ugly little Colorado town that we don't remember when the powers that be drove our fathers into the ground because they wanted safety and peace and food for their wives and children. We were organized labor because we had to be. We still have to be. When Chavez made the ridiculous request for a living wage and safety and food for his children, far too many of us laughed at the crazy Mexican and bought lettuce and grapes anyway.

He stood in the face of American displeasure and demanded that we begin to see his children in the same light we see our own. I'm proud to say I didn't buy any grapes or lettuce, and I never put a prefix in front of his name. It was not necessary for me to mark him as a "Latin Labor Leader", because union has to be blind to the differences between us. Smart media types who invent the tags that separate us are ignorant of the history that drove union and solidarity and organization. Chavez was a reminder of what we were. I hope picking is easy where he is. Make movies.

World War II is ancient history to most of you, but if you're over fifty it is still one of the hallmark events of your life. Every man, woman, and child on the face of the earth was involved. That fact alone still staggers me. In 1994 we land a battalion on some third world shore and all hell breaks out. The fact that the real impact of that event reaches to the end of the day is lost in the overwhelming gabble of the media. The Second World War was marked by the destruction of Europe, most of Asia, and the deaths of seventy million or so human beings. The figures are so unimaginable that you can be allowed some few moments of awe. One single battle that included only German and Russian troops resulted in two million deaths. In ten years in Viet Nam, America's total losses were sixty-five thousand.

Don't misunderstand me. I think that figure is an obscenity. The fact that two and a half or three million Vietnamese were also killed helps make war a horror in any perspective. This is not about the fact of war, but rather about the fact of American. From the very beginning of World War II, from the darkest fact of its beginning, none of us ever really doubted that we would finally overcome the Axis powers, as they were called. We were a simpler kind of people then. We had the amazing ability to believe that doing the right thing would win in the end. Our character as a nation was made from a hundred and eighty million citizens who, in spite of the nastiness of prejudice and cast hatred and all of the other goofiness to which humans can ascribe, still believed we were the good guys; and the good guys always win. It's absolutely true—we are the good guys, and the good guys always win. We've just forgotten how to tell ourselves that often enough to let our children believe it.

I learned about us in darkened theaters on a million matinee Saturdays. I knew who the bad guys were because the rules were laid out so clearly for me. When I got older and was less constrained to break rules than I was as a child, I still knew what the rules were. We were not about to traffic with the bad guys; we were the prop that held up the world. We still are. Bruce Willis knows it from the top of a towering building, standing on bleeding feet, and defying the villains; so does Dirty Harry Callahan, and the singer's bodyguard. So do the kids who are learning about the nature of evil and heroes during the new matinee.

I don't think we say it as well or as willingly as the old time film guys did. We seem to need to air our fear as fact so often that we are scaring our citizens to death. Lighten up. The world is not coming to an end, and it doesn't hurt to shout out some good news now and then. All those who believe that Billy Clinton is the Devil, please knock it off—movies?

My grandson bought school clothes this week. I guess everybody's grandson bought school clothes this week. When I was a kid my school clothes came from Wards or Sears, catalogue department, and were usually pretty straight ahead stuff—two pair or incredibly stiff brand new blue jeans, legs eleven inches too long (when I was a kid we rolled up big cuffs), four or five pair of socks and appropriate underwear and shirts. I had some choice about shoes, picking between the three available styles of great big, clunky, heavy brogans. There wasn't much passion in the buying and deciding because my choices were really limited. I never wore "tennis shoes" except in gym class, because everybody knew that a five dollar shoe that made feet sweat and was mostly canvas and rubber was not good for the feet. I'd imagine all this stuff cost about twenty-five dollars and would last until Christmas when part of my presents would be second semester clothes.

My grandson spent eleven million dollars and will have to buy again, probably next Tuesday. He bought two pair of five dollar tennis shoes that are bad for his feet and made out of mostly canvas and rubber and cost three hundred dollars a pair. He also bought two giant size training shirts (official NFL gear—price slightly higher than a down payment on a home) with matching shorts, t-shirt, wrist band, et cetera, ad nauseam. I was informed that the reason this stuff is so expensive is because it is real licensed goods authorized by the manufacturer. What does that mean?

This isn't really about my grandson's school clothes. It's about the strangest change in the free market system I've ever witnessed. They call the shirt a blazer—it's not. And when purchased with the shorts and the t-shirt and the wrist band, et cetera, ad nauseam, retails at the mall for between eighty and a hundred fifty dollars. In my travels I've found the same items for sale for about thirty dollars. I don't understand the reasoning of the marketplace. I mentioned this to my grandson, and he told me that since I had obviously been looking at bootleg stuff, I had to understand that the guy selling it for thirty dollars was stealing from the guy who sells it for eighty to a hundred fifty dollars. I asked my grandson who the guy that sold it for eighty to a hundred fifty dollars was stealing from—I got the same blank stare I got when I first talked to my grandson about three hundred dollar tennis shoes.

I don't see any major improvement in modern marketing. It doesn't appear that salesmen are any better or that products are any better or that people have lots more money to spend. It mostly appears as if the average IQ of the average buyer has slid seventy-seven points in the last twenty years. Don't be insulted—wake up. We keep talking about the national debt and the balance of payments and little children starving in Biafra. How about we just make the marketplace the same competitive proposition it was when I was a kid. If a guy can sell me a "blazer" and all that junk for thirty dollars, we ought to let him do it. And if a guy can make ten movies for two million dollars, we ought to help him do it. A hundred million dollar movie is as outrageous as a three hundred dollar tennis shoe. Make movies.

One of my favorite cartoons is a picture of a properly adorned preacher, surrounded by alter boys and assistants, frantically surveying mounds of money and jewels and other rich and glittering gifts. The caption under the picture reads, "Think. Think. What did I say?" Every so often I get the same wondrous response to something I write. Don't misunderstand, I almost never get anything that reminds me of money, but the mail swells and the phone rings merrily. I get some odd questions, and some great pats on the back, and an occasional invitation to a hanging. My own!

Last month I wrote my easiest stuff. Nothing very profound, just the fundamental belief that I hold that making my neighbors healthy and strong protects me and mine. I have roots in one of the groups of people who found their way here a miracle and rejoice in that fact every day. If I hold any particular power or franchise, I'm not aware of it. I hold no obvious political edge or financial wisdom, but I have learned how strong we are when we are in accord. The mystery that drives my life has carried me to all four corners of the globe. I have eaten from golden plates and dipped my naked fingers into the common pot with some fairly scurvy characters. I have an extra belly button I picked up in my travels, courtesy of a crazy trying to kill anyone, and more than a few nicks and pits in the front half of my shell. Like the common turtle I have learned that you make no forward progress until you stick your neck out. Way out.

Don't make the mistake of including me when you want to blast America and Americans. We are the cutting edge of the human experience and the hope of the rest of the world. Our citizen is from every corner of the planet and still more recognizable as an American from somewhere than any melted down hybrid. Our citizens speak every known language and follow every face God has ever shown us. Here we have that right, and the vast majority of us are willing to risk life, liberty, and our sacred honor to defend that right, for anyone in the world, anywhere in the world. We feed everyone we can reach and cry over lost dogs. We can be vain and head-strong and sometimes very stupid—but we are never stingy or selfish if we know who has a need for our strength and courage. This in spite of cowards who want to convince us the world is a fearful place and we must hide from our duty to the rest of humankind. Mankind's differing face is who and what we are.

Our enemies are sickness, both of the body and spirit, and ignorance and greed and fear and waste and cowardice. Those of you who are crying out for unity must understand that EVERY PERSON must link arms with you, or "unity" is only another odd club. If the world were on fire, we would all join hands to put out the flame. It is—make movies.

When you begin to get old, two odd things happen. The first has something to do with failed expectations. You become less willing to believe that everything will be all right. Failure is not only not a stranger to you, it's downright friendly. The old ignorance that kept you in the dark goes way. This new, slowly growing knowledge of all your failings replaces the blindness you used to mistake as a positive attitude. You develop the jaundiced view you remember your parents having about your love life or friends.

The second thing has to do with a slowly faltering step. You can no longer leap tall buildings at a single bound. This fact is way too slow in dawning on some people. You can spot the men by the odd way they begin to comb their hair over a shiny spot, and the women begin to laugh too brightly and quickly at things they secretly believe are stupid. The worst part of the way we treat our new knowledge is the way we pretend that we really don't know the difference between what's real and what's not. Most of us pretend that the terrible waste of resources on nonsense that surrounds us is the way things have to be. We don't want to look like we have learned anything by living. If we do, we have to admit we are getting older.

The deadliest duo in history are probably tobacco and booze. The terrible twosome destroy the lives of most of the people they touch. It's hard to imagine a human being who has managed to avoid the pain caused by a cancer death or an alcoholic father, friend, or lover; yet we spend the most horrendous amount of money selling both items to children who believe what we say because we have learned to say it so well. We make the consumption of both trash items the fast way to social acceptance. I think I've finally lived long enough to say that this "bud" is bullshit.

    I've done all kinds of things to make a living, and for the most part I've hurt very few people. But when I use the power of the word to sell bad ideas to the defenseless, I cross a critical line. I'm just an old guy who's reached the place in my life where I can begin to see what my careless use of this power has cost the ones I loved the most. You can do whatever you have to, but I think I'm done with it. Living is hard enough as it is without making it harder by pretending I don't know when someone is getting into trouble because I influenced them wrongly.

    We waste the best of us by jumping into things that are ill conceived and serve a small bunch of hustlers making a buck. We act like we can't tell the difference between public works and pork barrel. We act like we can save ourselves by walking over the less fortunate or less talented or lucky. We don't have to. Share a little. Make movies.

I pride myself on being reasonably level headed and responsible. I tend to keep both feet on the ground, my eye on the ball, my shoulder to the wheel and my nose to the grindstone. (Trust me. It was difficult learning to work in this position.) I am neither naive nor cynical nor Pollyanna nor foolish nor avaricious nor greedy nor anything that demands a one word label. (I'll admit to fat.) I have been all over the world, and I know to the core of me the difference between our America and what's number two. I may be the ultimate patriot. I think America bashing is the ultimate stupidity. I'm politically liberal and artistically conservative but am willing to let you be anything you want to be. I speak sagely about American values and freedom of religion and how stupid racism is and about how unreasonable being hopelessly poor or sick or disenfranchised is in our country. All in all, I can be a pompous jerk.

It's just before Christmas for me, and I get all misty-eyed and puffy-nosed and weepy and mellow at this time of year. I love everyone, especially my family, including the doofusses. This led to a lesson I got the other day. A young fellow called me wanting to buy a camera. We had to dicker because he wanted more camera than he had money (he got it), and I like to dicker. He lives in San Francisco, was born in Shanghai and came to our country with nothing, like most of us originally did. Nice guy to talk to. Great feeling for America, for all the popular reasons: freedom of speech—religion—whatever. Ours was a long and interesting conversation, and I really don't have time to recount it all, so I'm going to paraphrase a sentence or two and hope it's as powerful in the telling as it was in the hearing.

I'm a sucker for the season, and I had a sorry, wistful, teary-eyed concern for his being so far from home with no family. I'd asked if he was ever going home, and he said no. I allowed as how the loss of all those family ties must really be painful. There was a funny pause, and then he said, very softly, that what he had found in this country was infinitely more important than family—freedom. He could never go back. I haven't done a very good job of telling you how much I learned about us from this short conversation. There was no room for philosophy in the face of his conviction because he didn't give any less value to his family than I give to mine. He simply had a clearer understanding of how amazing the gift of self-determination really is.

Ours is the only country on the face of the earth where the quality of life is even a question. The question everywhere else is whether you live or die. It is very popular in some circles to talk about our decay and demise because our infrastructure is tattered. Try to remember that our infrastructure doesn't leave the bodies of starved, murdered human beings in the dirt. Rejoice—Rejoice—Rejoice. Make movies.

Writing about Christmas is a frustrating thing. Most of the time I can be more or less original in thought and execution. It feels like everything a person can say about Christmas has already been said, a thousand times before, by people who write better than I.

I have a distinct advantage over most people where Christmas is concerned. I've spent Christmas as an orphan, warrior, prisoner, lover, father. I've spent Christmas with no money and no hope, and I've spent Christmas's that in memory shine like diamonds and gold. I have never spent a Christmas watching my children starve to death.

This year the daily news is full of starving babies and murderous, subhuman brutes. I'm horrified when I discover by watching the news how little it takes to save thousands and thousands of lives. A regiment of marines and a couple of dozen attack helicopters, and the monsters murdering thousands of Somali children run away into the brush like the trash they are. Seems like an excellent use of marines to me. Seems like a great use of bags of flour and rice and corn and other things we pay farmers not to grow. People say Christmas is a season of brotherhood and hope for humanity and good cheer. Where were the marines for the last twenty years while thirty million starving someone-elses died? Brotherhood's a good idea, but this year in Somalia Santa Claus is wearing khaki camouflage, carrying an M-16, and riding a humvee.

Talk's cheap. If it seems I'm slightly far afield typing this on my new 386DX Acros computer with four megs of RAM and a 120 meg hard drive and Dos 6.2 and Windows 3.1 and

Super VGA—cost over a grand—after eating, personally, enough roast beef to match the total protein input of at least one hundred Somalis this week, it is as it seems. That's what Christmas is about. All of us, maybe especially me, need to be reminded that we live at the pinnacle of human experience in not only time, but place. We talk to God on a one-to-one basis and foolishly believe that He answers our prayers for electronic devices at Christmas time while ignoring the full third of humanity that lives—every day of their lives—like the Somalis live.

We only pass this way once. The truth is, we are the answer to the prayers of humanity's wretched poor, starving, oppressed. We have the power to save them—all of them. It's possible that Christmas will come for a million years no matter what we do. But Christmas will mean nothing until we do that which we are obliged to do. God bless us all.

I've played Santa for twenty years. I am a dead ringer for the old elf, and with my beard and hair whitened, I was the real thing for ten thousand kids. I loved the silly game and still have little kids insist that I am the "Old Man" when they see me in a restaurant at this time of year. My wife and kids seem to relish the game as much as I do, and my grandkids are convinced that I take out the sleigh and work late on Christmas Eve—best part of an otherwise checkered reputation. This is about learning from the game.

My friend, Jesse, is the kind of man I'd love to be. He watches the ads and buys veggies and meat in quantity for the kids' home in his area. He is honestly as charitable as I wish I was. He seems blind to the dirt and despair he walks through with arms full of food and clothing for people who are really down in spirit and luck. He gets no attention and would probably be astounded that everyone is not like he is. Don't mistake this as a cheer for him; he wouldn't want it or take it. His is the kind of charity that has no hook in it. He believes the Good Book and lives like it says. He is his brother's keeper and gives all of himself to Faith and Hope and Charity.

He asked me to be Santa for the kids at the county "special" school. This is the final hiding place for the hardly human. It is a repository for living tissue that defied the death most of us would wish them if they were ours. I'm not making too good a showing of myself here, am I? I was terrified. I am like a lot of people who don't handle some of life's horrors very well. These poor souls are damaged beyond the imagination. I was afraid that I would pull back in revulsion and make the already terrible life of one of these kids worse than it already was. I didn't know how to let Jesse down, and so I pulled on my best rig and became the real thing—belly, ho ho ho, and all. We arrived just after lunch when the kids usually had some free time. In more despair and panic than I can describe, I walked in and one of the counselors shouted, "Look who's here." There was little you'd recognize as a child in this room—but they knew that I was Santa Claus and that Santa loved them all—no matter what they looked like. After the birth of my children and grandchildren I got the best proof of God in this room I'd so despaired of entering. I was Santa, I DID love them all—and I have never done a better thing or had a better day in my life.

If Jesse had noticed my terror, he hid the knowledge from me, and we never spoke of it. But he gave me the chance to become the kind of human being we all want to be. I have never found myself afraid to reach out for another hand—or flipper—or whatever. Love one another. Make movies.

It's the time of the year when we should have hearts full of Christmas pudding and the like, but all I feel so far is dyspeptic. The troops are trying to penetrate a foul fog to land in Bosnia, and the goofballs in Washington have managed to do nothing that looks statesmanlike. I have the feeling that the fancy new Congress hasn't got a clue as to their real job—making the government work. It appears more and more that they think like freshman volleyball players—that the score is what counts. (Dear Congress: Balancing one's desire to flex one's muscle with the needs of the country is your real contract. Knock it off. Go to work. Remember "All God's Chillun" need representation, not just the money crowd.) I feel a Christmas rush.

Miracles come in odd sizes and appear at weird times. Most of us have a tendency to want fire, smoke, brimstone, and sulphur smells, but a miracle usually passes in a soft moment that we seldom recognize—a baby's birth, an answered prayer, a soft spring rain, fields of grain and grazing cows, all of the things that make us glad to be alive and healthy. We Americans have far more to make holiday cheer easy. We are as free of fear and anger as we allow ourselves to be. We must really blame ourselves for any lack of goodwill we feel for our brothers; no one can make you angry but yourself. For most of us it's easy. Put down your prejudice and hate. Reach out to the one who most needs your strength and care. Let the idea that the buck is the bottom line join all of the other really stupid ideas that mankind has latched on to from time to time. And remember, that no matter how high you stack it up, when you die you get in the box alone, empty-handed. I think that looking in the Bible for proof of your own worth and your neighbors' nastiness is like reading a novel for the "dirty" parts.

My miracle came from McDonald's this year. No, you cynical devils. I did not win the million dollar giveaway. Someone else did. AND THEY GAVE IT AWAY—ANONYMOUSLY. How about that for a miracle? It showed up on the fourth page in the local paper—less than a dozen lines—less than the number of lines dedicated to the menu at the Odd Fellows brunch. The mighty McD's was doing a game, Super Monopoly or something like that, and had allowed the possibility for three winners, odds of about ten billion to one, and someone won the game. Then the winner put the winning game in a manilla envelope and sent it to Saint Jude's Hospital.

Can you imagine the look on the face of the lady opening the mail when she discovered what she was holding? I wonder if she had a momentary thought of putting the thing in her pocket and becoming a millionaire. If she didn't think it, I think that's miracle number two. And if she did and turned it in, that's miracle number three. Sounds like a movie to me.

By the time you read this the holiday season will have vanished for another year. I imagine it comes as no surprise to you that I am a sucker for the whole Magilla. Every year I ask Santa for the same thing—that all of us, each and every one, share the blessings of God. My prayers are seldom more involved than that, but I want more for all of you than I've ever asked before. I wish you peace and joy and happiness, of course, but I want you to take care of one another. This simple idea seems far harder to achieve than any other. For one day take care of each other, and then do it again, every day.

Money—education—color—religion—politics—place in the pecking order—meaningless if you make them the reason you can ignore the pain of another. In this wide, wonderful world we are fast losing the ability to kid ourselves into believing that we are unique. If you can run over another because you have the odd notion that you are special, you ARE special; you are a jackass. Try not to get lost in the fact that I used an ugly expletive; trust that the one I want to use is far worse. The truth is now, as it always has been, that monsters roam the world. They are disguised as religious sects and political action groups and a thousand other "exclusive" gatherings. They are hiding places for the heartless and stupid and frightened.

For me the horror of the pain and the fear of my brothers—black, brown, yellow, red, white—is the hardest thing to face. All of your children are mine, and all of mine should be yours. The cost of acting otherwise is disaster. I know most men to be of good will. I know most men to be stalwart in the desire to make their family safe and secure. I have never found a healthy man who could spout the kind of filth that divides us. More importantly, I have finally found the truth of our real nature in this awful separation that robs us of our power. WE HATE BEING DIVIDED; WE ARE ALL FAMILY.

The statistics tell us that six percent of all of our white children live in dire peril, the percentage is far higher for our black children, higher still for our brown ones. Poverty crosses all of the lines that we pretend divide us, so does hard work and good citizenship and honor. We have let ourselves be deluded into thinking that the other guy is somehow responsible for the pain we all share. We are not lost to some invisible force; we are lost in the fear of others who are identical to us. I have met the real enemy—he is us. We must find a way to uncover our eyes and see the truth. Our problem is based on the simple failure of all of us to care for one another.

Faith—Hope—Charity—the profoundest ideas in the WASP ethic. The phrase, "And it came too pass," is the most common sentiment in the Bible; the parable of the Good Samaritan is the easiest to teach. Our pain will pass if we teach the parable. If you can't find the strength to help your brother, get out of the way and place the blame and the weight of your fear where it belongs, on yourself. Be of good cheer all you men of good will. Peace on earth. Make movies.

About once a year I get the odd urge to smack someone in the nose. At such times I take a few deep breaths and consider the following question: Is it worth thirty days in the slam to poke this jackass? To my great disservice it has too often been worth at least thirty days. I say this with no particular pride, and as an excuse I hold up my father and uncles who were terrible role models. At an early age I managed to learn the difference between the admonition to shut up and the request to stand up, but I also learned that suffering a bully was invariable worse than getting hit in turn. Sometimes you have to stand up.

It seems we have entered one of those times in our history when we are being beset by bullies on all sides. The right hates the left, the left hates the right, the middle is horrified and hiding their heads in the sand, the rich are making a fortune, and the poor are still voiceless and impotent because money talks. Our schools are graduating kids who can't read or write or understand who we are or where we come from.

Private militia are trying to decipher inscrutable codes on the backs of road signs. They hold secret meetings where they hand out pictures of abandoned railroad yards with the cryptic message that they will be used by a secret invading army to collect all the real God-fearing, true-hearted, ignorant, unwashed who are the real targets of the secret world power. Give me a break. I don't have any real hope of sugarplums or max-brotherhood or the like, but is it too much to expect a little quiet from all of the coo-coos?

Show me a freshman Congress type who is not already hustling his re-election, or a liar paying big bucks for a spin doctor (new word for specialists in lying, cheating, stealing) to try to rewrite every foolish sound out of his mouth. I hate the fact that the media has finally chosen to refer to the President of the United States by his surname and never call him Mister President, which is his due. If you are childish enough to believe that this particular Rhodes Scholar—dedicated politician—is the anti-Christ the right make him out to be, please compare his real nature with the pure souls they endorse. I have been unable to see the whites of anyone's eyes for ten years because of the mud in the air. Naturally, we are blameless because information means we print or broadcast every word from every source with equal abandon. I think that we are losing the truth game to the sound byte. We are the communicators and should be held to a higher standard. Let's print what they say and let the meaning trickle down.

We have to educate the ignorant and elevate the downtrodden and stop the giveaways. Stop the pork and make national job training for all of our citizens a reality, then the rest will take care of itself. We must build a new legacy for the children of the mine workers and foundry workers and auto workers whose jobs vanished after they built America. Stand up—make sense—make movies.

We haven't done bad for a collection of wretched refuse. When you use words like courage and dedication and inspiration to describe us and our founding fathers, you're hitting a wall that limits the language. Our founding fathers were reckless and foolhardy. They were card sharks and carpetbaggers running away from their own hanging. Their words were magnificent without being ponderous. "We hold these truths to be self-evident—"Four score and seven years ago"—"Give me liberty or give me death"—"Nuts." Language, language, language—words spoken in every language on earth, in every dialect of those languages, by desperate, happy, empowered, frustrated, slaves, freemen, rich, poor, dying, Americans. I think we've hit a low place.

I'm not Pollyanna. There is much stormy and dark in our character. We built this nation exploiting every new group of immigrants. The forests are gone, the red men have been pushed aside, the rivers have been dammed. That manifest destiny—that spreading from sea to shining sea—has long been accomplished. It seems to me we're way behind schedule in realizing the dreams of those monsters who got here first.

This is not about America bashing. I'm our biggest cheerleader, and time has taught me this infinite truth—that zero is the only natural number in nature and with every plus you get a minus. Founded in freedom, we brought millions to this country in chains or bondage. Millions of us have died breaking the chains and freeing the bound. We plundered a continent building a nation, and built a nation. Humanity learned how to organize and cooperate to build the greatest nation on earth and then let fear and stupidity jam us underneath Jim Crowe and McCarthy and Japanese internment camps. Each time we stumble and almost fall the integrity of our human nature picks us up, dusts us off, stands us on our feet, and compels us forward.

If I could lead you by the hand through history's papers and make the words of the early monsters as clear to you as they are to me, you'd understand that we are, indeed, one. There is no division between us—there can be no division between us. The only reason a division exists is because those of us who have the responsibility of telling America's stories to the rest of us have become cowards. Had George Washington, Abraham Lincoln, Patrick Henry, or some American colonel at Bastogne been afraid to say what they felt, there would be no America.

Klansmen are wrong—Muslim extremists are wrong—fanatics from the far right are wrong—fanatics from the far left are wrong. We are one. We are America. We can not survive without one another and history has already taught this lesson. We will survive. Each generation in turn has to swallow hard the bile of frustration and unrealized ambition, and then stand up and be Americans. Fight about it, cry about it, rage about it, glory in it—American. Make movies.

Do you think it's possible that every man, woman and child on this planet has an easy and immediate solution to the world's problems? I'm certain I have, and I'm positive you do. Be assured we will not agree on the solution. Marvelous thing about being a human being, we all look and smell and feel and think the same. It's odd that I say that, because I know people who are tenth generation Harvard graduates who function in a world I haven't a clue about. Trust me when I say they have no more understanding about what I am or where I come from. Between you and I, in spite of the fact that we are identical, I haven't the foggiest idea of what you're about.

The most significant part about being a human being is the sense of self-realization. No matter what class—cast—significant group—you think I'm a member of, I am still an individual. My attachment to class—cast—or group has a profound effect on me, but it shouldn't dictate my conscience or goals or attitudes about other people. Unfortunately, it does.

The tenth generation Harvard grad is a nice man, but he sees me from a position of such power and privilege that I'm little more than a cipher on the balance sheet of his world. For my part, I lump him with the monsters that seem to profit at every crop failure, disease, and war that has enriched the past nine generations of his family. If you live in Nicaragua, you think he and I are identically rich Americans. This is about prejudice.

When I was a kid there were only two kinds of people—cowboys and the other guys. There were white cowboys, black cowboys, brown cowboys, red cowboys. Forgive me, but I don't remember any yellow cowboys. I'm sure on the steppes of Mongolia they've got yellow cowboys. I saw myself as a cowboy and I was defined by my hat, hip hugging Levis, pointy toed Justin boots, and a steely eyed glint (the truth of my little porkiness had no bearing on my self-image). In the taverns and restaurants, on the fair grounds and stockyards of my youth, cowboys were only cowboys. I had to meet other people to see the differences between cowboys reflected in their eyes before I could perceive such difference. The cowboys didn't change, I did.

It took hard work for me to go back to being a cowboy. The other guys are only slightly less important than cowboys because they're not. (You see, even at that level an odd prejudice creeps in.) Bankers aren't cowboys, truck drivers aren't cowboys, airline pilots aren't cowboys, preachers aren't cowboys. Only cowboys are cowboys. (Except for really pretty girls who are all certified-real-authentic-first-original-cowgirls. I love cowgirls.)

Since all you have to do to be a cowboy is put on a hat, hip hugging Levis, pointy toed Justin boots and a steely eyed glint, I think that it would be easy for all you guys to change. I've worked way too hard relearning to be a cowboy, and I don't want to change anymore. If you don't think that you can change, buy a ticket to the rodeo. Make movies.

I try not to watch the Academy Awards. Whatever process the "Academy" uses to determine who is best at what only confuses me. I'm too good an audience to understand most of the mystical methods they use to judge the relative value of things. This doesn't mean that I resent the celebration, only that I think it has very little to do with making films. Perhaps it's like all of human experience; millions and millions of human beings live desperately and anonymously, while we record the history of the insignificant few.

I've had too many heroes in my life, whose names you would never recognize, to be impressed with the significant qualities of those chosen by historians. It seems to me that the truth of life is that all of our stories are the same. This is about Hale-Bopp and the thirty-nine new astronauts.

I've always been baffled by the people I've read about and known and loved who lived their lives as if every moment had been carved in granite by the finger of God. The truth of my life is that I've often stood, panting, in the center of a maelstrom of possibilities, without a clue. The thirty-nine new astronauts amazed me. I've lived as long as most of them, and I promise you, after studying a lifetime of human experience, I'm not about to eat an odd pudding, put a plastic bag on my head and hurl myself into the cosmos. I don't know what you could say to me that would convince me that's the way I should go. Maybe I'm missing something.

To be politically correct you have to embrace a whole new language. It has to encompass racism, sexism, history, the law, education, religion, and be so obscure that no one could, even by accident, discern the truth of what you're saying. I don't understand that language. What I say is what you get. I know God; I know Genesis; I know Darwin; I know Jew, Catholic, Protestant, Buddhist, Hindu, Muslim, white, black, red, yellow, four dozen shades of tan. I can't find any significant differences. Talented, beautiful, knowledgeable, well educated people from each of those groups have expounded at me in turn about the absolute certainty of their vision of the cosmos. They have nothing in common. It's no wonder that the Academy confuses me. I have to believe that God breathed life in me and expects me to keep breathing in and out until I can't handle it anymore. I hope I've got the guts to hang on if the world is coming to an end and I have to breath fire and vacuum for awhile. I think God made better than He knew. I know God made better than most of you know.

Let Hale-Bopp go its own way. Let all of life's prejudices go with Hale-Bopp. We can only talk to one another when we reach out and touch one another, and when we do that we discover how foolish waiting for the great space craft really is. I'm surrounded by people who are willing to embrace any possibility. I'm not that democratic. Some things are ridiculous by definition. I think the defining nature of foolish ideas are those that aggrandize you for the accident of your birth or your grandfather's luck in the stock market or where on this planet your soul landed.

I guess if someday some great ethereal purple mist lands at the city hall in Muncie and grants us all a world of peace and plenty with no work—no fear—no responsibility, I will have to apologize to all of you. Waiting for the purple mist makes no more sense than going with the thirty-nine new astronauts and Hale-Bopp. Make movies.

Ya Wanna Make A Movie?

Spring is finally here and I find myself remembering sounds and smells from the springs of my youth. I am far away from my beginning and much of what my memory saves so lovingly is gone. I have not heard a magpie yelling about how beautiful and manly he is for years, but the sound is in my dreams and bones. Pushing cows, or mending fence, or clearing water ditches marked the new coming of the sun, but from this end of my life even the new blisters and pain of ten hour days remembers sweet. I can't do the work any more. I envy the hard old men of my childhood who managed to stay tough and able until they were very old; for me failing parts are showing way too soon.

I am feeling the loss of a kid's strength and am surprised by how angry it makes me to grow old. I have been as independent as any man can be in our century. I have seen much of the world and leaped joyfully into harm's way more times than prudence would have allowed. It hasn't been enough. I have healthy children and beautiful, strong grandkids with the same sizzle in their eyes I hope was in mine, but I am finally the oldest among the family I cherished for so long, and I miss having the old man tell me what I should do. I can't find any sign of the boy I was in the mirror.

I have a hard time pretending that I don't mind falling apart. Frankly I'm furious about it but can't stop the process. On a scale of one to ten, my problems are about a two and a half, but they are my problems. I'm not writing this to lament this odd process of getting old. I am only relating the coming personal travail so that you will stop wasting time and get on about the joyful task of making your movie. I swear to you that I got this old in an hour. I have no idea when I began making my father's noise every time I got out of a chair, but I am suspicious that I have been doing it for a long time. I lament the passing of time unnoticed.

I have spent some time hashing out the facts of Mike Hirsch, and find him less than he wanted to be but more than he deserved. I managed to play the game pretty much the way I wanted, but am leaving much undone. I wish I could have stopped war and death and pain and fear, but I think we all wish for that power. I find that the most glorious things I accomplished always involved feeding the body or soul of strangers who needed help. I can't prescribe for you, but none of the awards or trophies I piled high are as impressive as the hungry kids I fed. I may no longer be able to leap tall buildings at a single bound, but I can still stop and help the ones among us who can't do it for themselves.

Some of you will never be able to see the hurting or needy—you will miss some great moments. We need the ones who can see because they are the real film makers. Life and movies are about how we take care of one another. Make movies.

When I started out I was a genius. I was tall and handsome, had unlimited potential, the world was my oyster. Oops. Some of you may be surprised to discover how few opinions I really have. No matter how I disguise them or rewrite them, no matter how I express myself, I still run into the limits of my vanished potential. It vanished in the undertow of failed expectations and squandered resources. It's only now, in retrospect, that I'm beginning to understand the disasters I visited upon myself.

This isn't about lack of intellect or drive or enthusiasm or a good heart. This is about the trip all of us have to make from nothing to something, from nowhere to someplace. The most profound thing I've discovered is that the most miserable kind of experience would be making this trip by yourself. In the words of Blanche Dubois (paraphrased), "I never would have made it without the support and kick in the butt from strangers." I guess in a way that's what our relationship is—yours and mine. I'm a stranger kickin' your butt. "Who are you to make such decisions?" you may ask. I'm you when you've spent all the power of youth and easy and stupid and lucky, and you have to live with what's left. I have three children, a mess of grandkids, a couple of friends, my wife (God bless her), and finally you.

I lived every day of my life chasing the big dream, shoving and pushing and scrambling, to carve great holes in history for myself. I have motivated and been motivated; I've plundered and been plundered; I have laughed and cried and jeered and cheered and watched the only resource on earth that matters finally slip away in the twinkling of an eye. I don't push and shove; I don't rage and fume; I don't plunder and pillage; I try to spend some part of every day helping you stand up. I've learned to be all kinds of things, none of them perfect, and I will likely never help you as much as you need or as much as I want. But it's the most important thing I've learned. You only get to do this once, and to paraphrase Spencer Tracy, "Learn your lines, then try not to stumble over the furniture."

The rules are simple—what goes 'round comes 'round. If somebody gives you all of the money you can possibly dream of to do what you want to do, they probably haven't shortened by one minute the amount of time you're going to have to spend learning the game you want to play. That's my opinion. I've discovered that the only resource I can't recover when I lose it is time. You can read about this game, you can dream about this game, you can stand next to this game, you can argue about this game, you can let it wash over you and around you and underneath you, and you're wasting your time until you get the words on paper, film in the camera, and a story told. I couldn't have become me without making every stupid mistake I ever made, but you quit kidding yourself by believing it's reasonable for you to make the same stupid mistakes I made. Go to school, go to church, fall in love, raise children, party, make movies.

Every once in a while I come face to face with a ghost from my past. When this happens I am usually stopped dead in my tracks for a moment. I am the type of human who lives most of his life in the here and now; and when the past jumps in, I have a hard time getting over it. I have reached the time of my life that welcomes a little forgiving and less stone throwing. I have been a student of the body politic and the insanity of the players since I was a child and have a general belief that most of the real bad guys get their just desserts. If history serves, we are about to see the comeuppance of a batch of liars and thieves. Of course, I am a Pollyanna type of guy.

Poor people and their vast problems are not about to destroy us. Neither are immigrants, legal or illegal—homo or any other kind of sexual—Japanese—car-jackers—crack addicts—black, whites, reds, tans, odd piebalds—or any of the other millions of things we are so fearful of. I have met the enemy, and it is ignorance that kills us. It is a mindless—ruthless—destructive thing that will sooner or later make a craven coward out of the strongest of us. Sadly it is hard to defeat and impossible to confront without the help of someone else. Sharing one's own ignorance is made fearsome by our inability to share with one another. We try to be all things to all men and fail. The truth shall set you free.

Until you can look in a mirror and see the real man or woman looking back at you, coming to grips with your own fear is impossible; and the vast majority of people never have to make that kind of confrontation. More is expected of you. You are the communicator. You are the one who defines the reality of life for the majority, who must take your word as truth and act on it. If you choose to be a thief or liar no one will know except you. The time comes to most of us when the demon will step up and make his presence felt. If he misses you, you can run for Congress as a reform candidate and scare little old ladies to death.

This is not about the right and the left and the middle and the guy in the back, it's about how prepared you are to know the truth when it steps up to you. You must know the difference between smoke and mirrors and not be dissuaded from the real game by the disguise the self-interested will dress their own agenda in. Don't be so quick to jump on the bandwagon with the loudest—make sure you know who gets paid when we all march in this particular parade. Tell the truth and make certain the enemy is in sight.

Communicator—great job. Doesn't pay much but makes the view in the mirror a pleasure. (The ghost was "Tail Gunner" Joe McCarthy, and he had turned into Newt and Jesse and The Boys; and we were all standing in the same old line.) Truth first—make movies.

I got my first camera when I was about five. It was an old Voightlander folding camera, made a 6x7 negative. It used one of the funny old film sizes that doesn't exist anymore or 2x3 inch sheet film. By today's standards it would hardly qualify as a photographic instrument. It had zone focus markings on the bellows side rail and for critical focus it had a built in ground glass. Taking pictures with it was something of a chore. No built in meter, no reflex viewing, no auto wind. Definitely no auto focus. No nothin'—just a spectacular little lens and a light proof box full of film. The amazing thing about the old camera is that, after forty years, some of the best pictures I ever took in my life were taken with it.

Most old guys become increasingly incoherent as they get out of touch with the real world. I'm probably no different. We all have a father who makes life style noises that are so foreign to us and so redundant that we get tired of listening. I hate the idea that I'm becoming one of those old guys. I think the truth is that as you get older all of the things that you think you really know and understand break down, fall apart, and become so much rhetoric. Truth, however, may be fundamental, and for that reason, every old guy you run across who feels compelled to wax profound about something sounds like he's waxing about the same thing. Aside from some cowboy stories, that old camera is the best example of everything I know.

In these times you can take your automatic, gas powered, chain driven, atomic energy efficient, twenty-five times zoom powered lens, phenolic body, super camera, jump out of an airplane with it in your hand, set it on automatic, drop it, and have it take two hundred and fifty perfectly exposed pictures of nonsense all the way to the ground. If it doesn't bounce and breaks into a million pieces, you can then replace it for $1.85. The two hundred and fifty shots cost you less than that to process, including the film. I know I'm exaggerating, but forty-five years ago just buying film was a major undertaking. You processed it yourself and exposed film according to rules passed from photographer to photographer and could spend three days shooting twelve pictures. No wonder some really extraordinary pictures were taken by an eight year old boy.

You couldn't take a picture by accident. You literally had to load your film in the dark. You couldn't afford to shoot ten thousand worthless pictures a year and throw them in the desk drawer, because it was way too expensive. The nature of the craft demanded a monstrous discipline. (There's that word again.) If you didn't do it by the numbers, you didn't do it at all. Creativity, education, point of view, even political necessity can affect the ethic of this thing we do, but you can't avoid or change the discipline.

Shabby film work because you are too lazy or too irresponsible to do it right is not artistic. It's only shabby film work. Make movies.

When I was a kid I made the greatest noise about the things that made the least difference. I passioned loudly for causes that were remarkable and safely untouched by my efforts. It is just as well since most of the real answers to the problems I attacked so busily proved to be far too complex for my eager, enthusiastic, blind approach. The failure was less in quality of presentation and zeal, than pure unbridled ignorance of all sides of the issues. I was moved by the wonderful youthful assurance that a frontal assault was the best approach. I have slowly learned the difference between shut up and stand up. I have many scars to prove the lessons.

Like all creatures of great passion and zeal, I was blessed with a gross resistance to the possibility that I could be wrong. I have learned that a certain amount of bullheadedness is necessary if you are going to make the trip to adulthood, but it is only bullheadedness after all. The lucky ones among us are those who take the fewest hits in the head by the wiser ones trying to get our attention. In turn, I have fallen in love, blindly and badly, with the wrong women and causes. I have broken the hearts of those who loved me first and best and the most unselfishly. I have ridiculed wiser, better men than I will ever be, and left undone things I should have done. I search my heart and past for sins that smack of mean spirit or small heart, and while I could be kidding myself, I find that I was more foolish than vain or cruel. I have often wished for a second chance. Truth is, we only go this way once.

The next is not meant as advice, only a possible way to skip the stupid things I've done. If the best answer you can fathom to a social problem involves attacking the powerless, it's wrong. If murder by any name is part of the answer, it's wrong. If the best test for your theory is the blind support of "your kind of people", it's wrong. If the answer would destroy you if you were the problem, it's wrong. If you believe you are immune from the fall out of the cure you suggest, it's wrong. We come from all over the world and are more astonishing for our sameness than our differences. The real enemies are those who are not able to change.

I have learned to love by being loved. I have learned to care by having others care for me. I have seen the new light in my children's eyes, and buried the first ones who looked at the same light when it was new in mine. I have waded hip deep in bloody war and mourned the loss of friend and enemy. The least lost among this brotherhood I have discovered we are is the same as the most lost. You are the ones who are called to communicate. The stories you tell must always be true. I have met the enemy, and he is us when we are stupid or uncaring. Make movies.

I have come to the conclusion that we are, for the most part, a really odd kind of creature. The best current guess is that we number about four billion, and each of us is convinced that he has the answer. It is becoming very clear to me that I don't even know the question. George Carlin did a concert in beautiful downtown Muncie this week, and the normal collection of religious types wrote letters to the editor of what passes for our local paper insisting that he deserves to be boiled in oil. He probably doesn't care.

I am only astounded that they would buy tickets to see him. I have been watching him for thirty years and have always expected the coo-coos to yell about what he has to say. I think he is a lot angrier now than when he was a kid, but then so am I. The desperate seem more so now, and I have more trouble seeing any answer. It surprises me because I know that most of the disaster everyone screams the loudest about is hogwash. We have an amazing capacity to live past the most horrendous happenings without letting any memory of what transpired alter our future actions. It probably has something to do with the fact that we hate looking bad. In the nineties almost everyone I know would rather lose than look like they didn't know what the game was. I want to know what I'm messing up.

Reagan and Bush—Clinton and Gore—Beavus and Butthead, they all have about the same real impact on anything that really matters to most of us. We seem to drive ourselves crazy mouthing the same platitudes and waxing sadly about how the future is bleak and mankind is doomed. If it's true, we can't affect the situation with all the screaming and yelling, and we'd scare fewer little old ladies if everyone would just calm down. I'm positive that we would all be better served if we tried to fix the closest thing to us; at least we'd spend a lot less time fomenting about things that we are not able to change.

I find myself writing about how tough it is for most little guys to make it, and lamenting the difficulty. Truth is, that's what makes us good at what we finally do. Some people read what I write as an excuse for failure or an apology for how hard the work is. They misinterpret. I want the new guy to understand that this is a monstrous way to make a living, even when you have all the tools to do the job. It is impossible if you try to cheat the ethic or discipline of the craft. I don't care much about what you want to say, there's room for plenty of disagreement among and between us. I hate watching people fail to make sense of what they say because they are in over their heads. You can learn to write, or shoot, or make music; the key word is learn. Most of us only get a few slim chances to try. Damn shame to waste it because you don't know how. Make movies.

If you can tell the difference between good and evil or the bad guys and the good guys when you go to a movie, please raise your hand. Now, how many of you realize that the actors are not the real thing? If so many of you are so smart, why do all the kids in the theater really believe that Wesley and Woody are basketball hustlers? How come everyone in Indiana and Kansas and South Carolina act like the "'hood" is next door to them?

I once climbed on a "freedom" bus with a bunch of guys who had just found out that everyone wasn't being treated the same in this country. We were terrified and threatened and yelled at and persistent. For ten years the passion of normal people, black and white and tan, flew in the face of a few mouthy and not very bright oddballs who had to hate someone. In spite of the crap you are hearing today, we made a hell of a difference. Maybe the proof is hidden in the fear that famous restaurant chain copped to in an instant when their dirty laundry hit the front page. The truth is that we really don't like bigots and haters much—white or black or tan or yellow or red.

Things are still not right. A part of our neighborhood of Americans still has a real hard time getting a fair shake in too many places. The terrible waste of humanity that finds themselves trapped in poverty and ignorance is a blot on what we really are. In spite of what the stingy and ignorant say, we have an obligation to fix things in the blighted corners of our "'hood". More importantly, we can best make use of them and ourselves by making certain that everyone gets to learn about life, liberty, and the pursuit of happiness. The ultimate stupidity is making the guy without a chance responsible for the state he's in.

We are the communicators. We are the ones who spread the word to the rest of us. If we waste our precious resources painting the same bullshit picture over and over, nothing changes. Bad movies are only bad movies when you know the difference. When you are a child or just unread or unlived, movies become the world. Watts is still in L.A., and the "Green" is in Chicago, and they don't belong in our "'hood". But they are not all of what black and white and tan and yellow and red Americans are about.

The same old freedom bus leaves at the same time every day, for the same reasons. The same children of good will are still riding it, but we act like it's gone forever. A cheap thug is the same kind of bum whether he is white or black or brown or cop or politician or movie maker. I think the truth can make a difference, and the truth is that most of us hate the idea that anyone lives badly. Brotherhood—make movies.

I think something's wrong with us. I'm certain that I don't do anything that I do for money's sake. You must understand that I don't punch a time clock or check in with anybody or go to a particular place every day, and I never have. In my whole life I've never had a job. I should probably amend that to say that I've never wanted a job, and so since I was twenty years old the only name on my paycheck was mine. I write it—I cash it—I spend it—everything. Sometimes this is wonderful. When I'm right and everything I'm touching is turning to gold, it's rewarding and thrilling and exhilarating and all that stuff. However, when I'm wrong, life can be hell. The truth is, in a lifetime I've been more wrong than I've been right.

I do what I do because I love the game, and what's more important, I love the game on a daily basis. If I go forward a little, then backwards a little, and create a little, and get a couple hours of good conversation, and rare roast beef, and a hot shower, and eight hours sleep, and a kind word from somebody who loves me, my life is perfect. If you gave me a hundred million dollars, I can't imagine it would be any better. For me, life is not about house and car and things and stuff. In fact, the hustle for the material things to do the work is as much fun as the work itself. Did you ever wonder if it was possible to give Francis Ford Coppola enough money so that he wouldn't have to hock his house to finish a movie? I understand that.

Films aren't made by people who have lots of money, because if you are a film maker, you can't possibly have a lot of money. You'll notice I said "film maker" not actor, director, banker, doctor—just film maker. The work will keep you broke. The only way to successfully make a movie is to go plunder the guy who thinks a bank account is important. Isn't it sad that nothing else is ever important to those kind of people? Their attitudes are so pervasive that the only way most of us can motivate the youngest of us is by talking about money. It's stupid. If I cared about money, I'd have some, and I don't. I can go get it from guys who think making a profit on the work is the same as working.

Please don't misunderstand me. I don't think for one minute that there's anything wrong with being an investor and prudent and keeping your eye on the ball, your shoulder to the wheel, etc. I'm only trying to explain this compulsion to produce. I'm not stupid about it. I don't waste my time or my resources on projects that are so speculative or ambiguous that I can't forecast a conclusion. There is nothing liberal about my artistic nature. When every project you're involved in has the potential to require all of your resources, financial—emotional—spiritual, you become very conservative about what you want to waste your time on. That's why I say I think we're wrong about the way we motivate. Life is not about money—ever—it's about playing the whole game every day. Success is a journey not a destination. Make movies.

I love circus. More now than I did when I was a little kid. I think all the obvious stuff thrills me—lights, noise, music, costumes, animals—everything. My very first memory of circus is my first memory. I had to be less than five, and some adult led me by the hand across a frosty vacant lot in the early morning to watch one of the great traveling shows raise its big top at dawn. A herd of elephants unloaded the monstrous railroad cars and slowly, with massive dignity, erected a magical city where before there had been nothing. Men yelled and screamed and hollered, and roustabouts drove stakes in the ground and raised towering poles and drug menagerie carts and fed wild animals; and in the midst of all this noise and insanity, the elephants did what they had to do with calm and dignity. I remember standing as they went by, close enough to touch, taller than I could see, and smelling wonderful. I can still hear and smell them after fifty years.

Ringling Brothers and Barnum and Bailey, Clyde Beatty, Porter Brothers, Polk, Circus Vargus—any of them—put up a placard, and I'll seek them out. The smallest show I ever saw was wonderful. The biggest show I ever saw transcended rare roast beef, sleep, money, and sex. It seems that some kinds of magic are greater than others.

I know people who think elephants stink and that circuses are too noisy and that popcorn and peanuts and bad hot dogs will make you sick or ruin your future or steal you from the church. I think they're nuts. God would love circus. It must be the closest thing to creation—in the beginning He put down straw.

Magic is expensive. You can't build a circus in ninety days.

You can't pretend a circus. You can't dream a circus. You study and practice and invent and create and work your ass off. It is the ultimate collaboration. You learn to fly when an old flyer teaches you, and you learn to clown when an old clown teaches you. An old lion tamer teaches you how to train new lions, and an old roustabout teaches you the rhythm to drive stakes. You have to learn it. You have to practice—practice—practice. And the magic happens when, from inside you, comes the way to make it all better. You can't throw away what went before because if you try, whatever you have left is not circus.

Making movies is a lot like circus. My second memory must be a movie because every cell of my body is full of old movies. The new stuff is wonderful, but there wasn't one single morph effect in Casablanca. Make movies.

I really hate it when I sound like I have nothing positive to say about anything. I'm not really as cynical as some of what I write sounds. The reason I write this stuff at all is to give an up stroke to the new guys. When I started playing this media game, things were just as hard as they are now. The power structure was as resistant to new blood as it is now and harder to deal with because there were a lot fewer jobs. The facts less angered than frustrated me. In addition, I lacked the kind of sophistication it took to get along with the many kinds of people it takes to make up the media community. In that sense, at least, the modern media education gives the new guy a leg up. (Please—guy just means person to this old man. I may be a sexist pig, but not where the work is concerned.) The point I'm making is simple—then, as now, no one got an easy or free ride unless their dad owned the company. My old man would have hired outside just to keep me honest.

From the technical side of the business, the modern new guy has another advantage. It takes a lot more hands to do the job than it took then. My evil twin side keeps telling me that you kids are not as smart as we were, and that's the reason it takes so many of you to do the job. I have to be fair. I may not have been any smarter, but I was lots tougher. In the whole world not one single communication arts school existed. Every single person in a crew started the same way—by pushing a broom.

I don't remember anyone having to hire a janitor as long as they could hire a kid who would do anything to belong. You got ahead the old-fashioned way. You were abused and exploited and taken advantage of and generally treated with no respect. The wonderful thing was the feeling you had when you earned the respect that you got.

It appears that today's "new guy" comes to the trade with the feeling that making film is easy or automatic. Nothing could be further from the truth. In spite of what your professors told you, between the word and the deed is the art. This game has far less to do with what you think you know than with what you are willing to endure.

Every year for over twenty years the "art" schools have graduated twenty-five thousand T-Com Majors. There are still less than a thousand people on the face of the globe really capable of making a feature film. The quality it takes to organize and muscle the resources necessary to make a film cannot be taught, only learned. After thirty years of watching the best players play this game, and playing as hard as I could when I could, I'm still in awe of the people who really do what I talk about. Make movies.

No matter how you feel inside, you are not an ancient fisherman just because you have seen *The Old Man And The Sea*. No amount of excitement makes you a fast gun after seeing *The Outlaw Josey Wales*. No matter what you wish, the lady in the rubber cat suit didn't really lick your face. Movies don't make you any taller or more handsome or smarter or richer. They do suspend reality for a time and make it possible for you to dream of doing the wonderful kinds of things the actors are doing on the screen.

Just because you have been watching the flickering images pass before you doesn't mean you are a film maker. In our society we are subjected to the film image from the cradle to the grave. Perhaps the myth that making a movie is automatic and easy gets its start in that fact. The old saw about familiarity breeding contempt fits here. It all looks so easy. By the time we have begun to date seriously, we can usually speak every line of our favorite movie along with the actors, but that is a trick of memory, not genius. Being appreciative of someone else's talent and skill is not the same as having that talent and skill. The truth is that while good ideas and good intentions and talent are the most worthless commodities on earth, they are often the rarest.

Anyone can put film in a camera and point it. It is science, not genius, that makes the image appear. You have to match real talent and an immense amount of time and effort to the camera to get a cameraman. Writers are much rarer and harder to find; so are sound men. Why is it so difficult for people, who accept the fact that they will never run a nine second hundred yard dash, to accept the equally valid proposition that making a movie demands a magnificent talent and discipline? The saddest conversation is the one a film maker has with a rank novice who has the automatic genius that comes with complete ignorance of the subject about which he waxes so profoundly.

The wonderful thing about the film experience is that it gives everyone the chance to express whatever genius they carry around inside themselves. You don't need a hundred million dollar budget to say some really wonderful things. But if you believe that you can become a Sam Peckinpaugh or an Alfred Hitchcock without spending a million tortured hours learning your craft, you are only watching movies. After a hundred or so years, the basic movement of camera and subject are not really a matter of great artistic interpretation. The rules of composition are academic and demand a real understanding that best comes without film running through your hands at a couple of bucks a foot. Education is cheap. Most of us only get a few slim chances to try. Learn how first. Make movies.

When a ship struggles to lift itself upon the coming swell, just for a moment, time stands still. It happens every single time. At that moment the contest is always in doubt; do you climb up the coming sea or founder and sink? No matter how large or small the ship is, no matter what the weather is like, the fact of that contest is so fundamental to the reality of sailing that it dictates a rhythm that lasts a lifetime. Grown men leap instantly awake from deep sleep at the smallest break in the tempo. Any change in the basic pattern of that contest is a portend of disaster. Having discovered that ebb and flow of life and death at an early age made me a better human being.

Don't misunderstand me. The contest is real, but experience and education make living with the potential peril common and easy. Sailors learn to wait until a reaction is necessary before they worry about the continuing game between ship and sea. They keep the ship healthy and in a state of good repair by constantly reviewing equipment and technique and proper reaction to the unthinkable. Going out of sight of land's end makes no sense if you can't navigate. Making your first attempt at sailing during a gale constitutes insanity. You can read every book ever written about the sea, and chances are, you'll drown trying to overcome the things you don't know. I feel an analogy coming along here.

This is about the rhythm of making films. We all have to learn something about the craft in order to say what we mean on film. I think it may be the hardest thing an artist can do. In almost every other form of human expression there is room for skidding around the fundamental technique, but not in film craft. Allegory becomes mystery if you have a lousy grasp of the reality of film's ethic or discipline. It has long been popular for American film students to adopt some odd European film coo-coo or another as an authority because the student can't make sense of the coo-coo's work. If you have to explain every scene to every audience, it is less art than bullshit.

I bitch about film content all the time, but faulting the technical quality of American film makers is ridiculous. I lament the fact that the bottom line has become the most powerful force in the process, but we make the best empty movies ever made. Even that small criticism is foolish because film for the sake of pure entertainment is the very best use of the art. My real complaint is that too many budding film types destroy themselves by biting off a movie project that is best compared to launching your first twelve foot yawl during a hurricane. Make a lot of little films that have something to say. It's the fastest way to learn the craft. Spend money as if you had to earn it. Make movies.

I still see with a photographer's eye. I can't remember the time before I became a shutterbug. My first camera was an ancient and beautiful Voightlander with an amazing lens and an odd film size that doesn't exist anymore. It was a view camera and required a dedication to procedure that kept the shooter honest. I'm still amazed that some of the best pictures I ever took I made before I was ten years old. The process developed what the old time cameramen call the "third eye". The squint and shoot experience was still fifteen years in front of me when I had my first news shot published; I was nine.

Science has discovered and proven that the human brain is divided into two halves reasonably designated right and left hemispheres. The right-handed human being engages the left side through his right eye and the right side through his left eye. The left side of the brain is the pragmatic, mechanical side and exhibits little creativity. The right is the creative side. It's odd that most film shooters only close their left eye and squint through a reflex view finder. Unless you make a real effort to acquire some view camera experience, the chances are remote that you will ever realize your creative potential. It's odd that most right-handed shooters cannot focus at all when trying to view through their left eye. This is the creative side and doesn't handle the process of photography well alone. The quality of your work should make a quantum leap if you will learn to see with the "third eye".

I know this sounds like voodoo, but trust me, the difference is amazing. The ability to see the most artistic display is handicapped without this small skill. There is abundant proof available if you need verification of this odd fact. The happiest proof is in the shooting after you play the two-eyed game for awhile.

At the most professional level, framing a shot is a process of open end viewing. The cameraman only uses his reflex finder to establish the parameters of the shot. The scene is laid out with both eyes open and makes use of both sides of the brain. Hence, the "third eye". Most new guys shoot through the lens in the fashion of documentarians and botch more film than they should because they are not seeing with any real artistic control. You can argue back and forth if you want to, but try paying more attention to the whole scene before you start peeking at it and watch the results. Better yet, buy an old graphic four by five camera and shoot some stills. It will make you a better cameraman.

If you take a backwards step and shoot some really old-fashioned shots, it will help you... make movies.

I spend a lot of time thinking hard learning things that seem simple. When I was a kid I knew about all there was to know and was hard to teach. I've come to the age that allows me to be far less wise. The changes that come about in a lifetime occur so slowly that most pass unnoticed. Most people never get the chance to just sit and reflect long enough to make sense of them. I have been unlucky enough to find a lot of time on my hands for a year or so, and lucky enough to get the opportunity to find me here, and remember where I've been.

Trust that I still find the world a wonderful place, with room for all types and hues of people, in spite of those who take it upon themselves to make theirs the only correct shade of man. I still find that people of good will outnumber the shabbies that make life so hard. Hirsch's first law states that since nothing can change the basic nature of a bigot or a jackass, letting them shape how you believe—or travel—is a waste of time. You only get to do this once. Dwelling on the terrors you can't change only keeps you from doing the good you can, and profits the haters and mindless who see your anger as proof of their power.

This is about Hirsch's second law; should be the first law, but for the unfortunate plethora of bigots and jackasses that clutter an otherwise wonderful world. The most worthless commodities on the planet are good ideas, good intentions, and talent. In a world of five billion souls the feeling that you are unique can get between you and where you want to go. I have watched men in this game destroy themselves by using resources to serve millions, for the aggrandizement of ego. If you approach this craft with the confidence that you have a talent that surpasses good judgement and education, you're doomed. The simple fact that nothing will insure success like knowledge and practiced skill is hard to swallow when you're very young and full of juice, but the truth is that most failure is self-generated.

The greatest film makers in the world are those who learn to trust that you can't get first class results until you can afford first class help—producers, writers, directors, and maybe most important, actors. I have seen wonder from a non-reflex Bolex and crap from a BL-4. In the computer game they say "shit in—shit out". Since the only one in the world designed by God to bullshit you is you, a judicious application of humility will go far in making the dream you dream come true. Don't misunderstand what I'm saying. You have to try this thing in order to make good, but the first major attempt at this can destroy you when you find yourself grafted to a horrendous piece of crap that you must finish.

If you have no film school, get some. If you are not a photographer, become one. Don't assume that there is anything easy or automatic about this craft. No one sets out to make bad films, but trust that your first effort will more resemble the worst thing you've ever seen than the best. Most of us have very little chance of becoming the next genius in this art of ours, but killing yourself in the process of proving you are the exception to hard work and exercise of prudent judgement is silly. Give yourself the best chance you can. Learn—Learn—Learn—and then make movies.

My new grandson is the most extraordinary child ever born. I know I can say that without fear of contradiction because, if you knew him, you'd surely be as impressed with him as I am. He is exceedingly handsome with the clear light of a magnificent intelligence shining in his eyes. All in all, a most amazing child. Or maybe not. When I see him my vision is obscured by this great thundering heart pounding in my chest. It's like having a new puppy—Mercedes Benz—girl friend—Arriflex.

Having grandsons is like making movies. It's hard to imagine the next one being as good as last one (sometimes they're not) but the difference is what makes life interesting. Being a grandfather is a collaborative effort requiring a minimum input from a daughter and/or son and the appropriate opposite, and some support from your distaff. The major collaboration is with other grandfathers who are willing to let my grandson be the most extraordinary human being ever born as long as I let their grandson, in his turn, be the most extraordinary human being every born.

Had a verbal fist fight with people who are not aware that film making is a lot like being a grandfather. Please believe me when I tell you that no one appreciates its collaborative nature more than I. Good script writers, good cameramen, good sound men, first class cable pullers, pretty girls, grand vistas, car crashes, ugly aliens, and high class financiers all collaborate to make movies. BUT—I still insist that no matter how collaborative the effort, someone must be the boss. I've never heard Spielberg referred to as "Spielberg-Jones-Maxwell-Smith-Rodriguez". Collaboration ends where the boss has to make the final decision. Artistic autonomy is not a luxury or an impossible dream. It is rather a necessity for a film maker. Autonomy without compromise may be impossible, but if I'm to be hoisted I would prefer that the petard be my own. You young guys have a lot more practice than I do at standing in line. When I was a kid, there were lots fewer lines and fewer people silly enough to insist that everybody had to line up. Real independence is going to be very difficult for you.

The hardest thing to be in today's world is "wrong". For some reason our society has decided that being wrong equates to being immoral, unworthy, stupid, disgusting, over weight, smelly—how many adjectives do you need? Truth: wrong is only wrong. Consider the poor turtle who makes no forward progress until he sticks out his neck. I have never seen a turtle without chips and nicks and thumped places on the leading edge of his shell. Give yourself a break—take a chance—take a shot—stick your neck out—and if you're wrong, do it again. Make movies.

I was going to start this thing with a paragraph from the dictionary—one of those film beginnings where the film maker uses the definition of a word to begin his story. I have not done that because I don't have the word space available for the ploy. This is about entitlement and you will have to finally define the word in your own way.

The Pros and the Cons are fighting a small war in Congress over the way they want to define the word. One side thinks the other side is trying to prolong the life of ancient pork by trying to destroy their far seeing—all powerful—vision of the future, and vice versa. I am not writing a new thing when I remind that one man's trash is another's treasure. I dread any political group that is professing to be driven by the only truth. Zealots are probably best used to make dead-to-the- last-man stands in forgotten wars; a prophet's words are usually best in the retelling anyway. When we finally find the way out of our dilemma, we will discover that we all have to give up something that hurts someone we love. Truth is, we are going to have to make a hard decision about our own entitlement or have our whole balloon burst from the internal pressure.

What the hell does this stupid diatribe have to do with making movies, you ask? We have the same problem in spades. I have said in the past that I am a lousy critic because I love everything I see on the screen. The pure process of film making is so difficult that I relish everything but the stupid formula crap of a cynical, lets-make-a-buck, hack. They usually show what they are by the script written in four letter words with yellow crayon. I am sometimes less than thrilled by the newest giant who has just sold a trillion tickets, because for me the bottom line is not the best test of a film. I am horrified by the two hundred million dollar artist. I think the use of enough money to make two hundred films to aggrandize one jackass is obscene.

I am not against using the new technology and pushing the envelope from the inside, but when thirty-five thousand children die of starvation every day, it is the ultimate act of cynical pride to waste so much resource for the petty thing they make. We are surrounded by human beings who are facing lives of real desperation. They watch the lifeline they call hope, and we call entitlement, vanish before them. We are pouring billions down the rat hole of pride and greed that is marking what some of us call progress. In the name of thrift we are manufacturing a permanent underclass in this country. We throw the least able to defend themselves on a pyre of rhetoric, while in this industry we throw away enough money on bullshit to finance day care until the end of time. The reality that two hundred million dollars saves Medicare for all of those Americans who have only that resource to sustain them in their old age should have some significance in how we use what we have. Make sense—make movies.

My youngest brother's daughter got married on the twenty-seventh day of July. I will remember her anniversary easily as it coincided with the thirty-fifth anniversary of my wife and me. We didn't go to the wedding. This is not about a family feud or uncaring relatives or any of the other things that make good soap opera. This is about being too old and broke up to handle a thirteen hundred mile drive. It's odd to have finally come to the point where I dread jumping in the car and driving anywhere.

In the forty years or so that my wife has been my girl, one great joy in our life was filling the gas tank and running it dry as many times as we could between things we had to do. My heart still wants to travel, my head still takes me to places I've been, but my body won't stand the pain. I think that parts of getting old are hard to take but losing wanderlust might be the worst.

I have a friend who's visiting his sister in Pueblo, Colorado. He made the trip from San Jose, California, and is looking forward to sitting around doing nothing. In my last phone conversation with him I gave him an itinerary of two million places (I may have exaggerated) he could visit within a hundred and fifty miles of his sister's house that beggar description. Colorado, whether mountain or desert, is a marvelous place to wander. I think he may live long enough so that he only regrets the things he didn't look at. I know I have.

No matter how odd some of my articles appear, they are all about using the freedoms we take for granted to make movies. We probably live in the only country on earth where you can set your mind free and follow it anywhere it leads. I don't know the New England states—I don't know Nova Scotia—I've never been to Mackinac Island—I miss them as much as I enjoy the memories of the places I have been. You only get to do this once, and you get in the box alone. If memory must last for an eternity, it would be sad to be plagued by the regret of things you didn't do.

Film is ultimately about having something to say that drives you. A vision that fills your mind so clearly that it has to be shared. Waste gas—don't waste time—make movies.

Don't get too cynical. On one hand we have film guys sneering at electronic production and post, and on the other hand we have tape guys insisting that film is too expensive and tape is just as good anyway and HDTV will blow film out of the water, etc., etc., etc.

All you guys get a grip. For the first time since 1930 an independent film maker can expect to make a living expressing himself. The real truth is probably somewhere in the middle of the arguments—but—right now the fastest way to superior video quality is to start with film. When tape aficionados cry about film cost, the obvious retort is an allusion to NBC, ABC, CBS, Fox, Podunk Broadcasting, who all use film to generate the primary image of their most important shows. However, when you're paying the star eighty thousand dollars a show, the co-star sixty thousand dollars a show, eight supernumeraries twenty thousand each per show, film's cheap. Of course, when you have a forty-five hundred dollar budget to make a fifteen minute film telling the employees of Acme Manufacturing please-don't-swim-in-the-hydrochloric-acid-vat, film can get pretty expensive.

I'm not certain you can really tell the difference between 16mm and 35mm when broadcast at less than three hundred lines; I'll let you techies worry about it. The reason for this noisy little essay is this: I have good friends with million dollar post suites that include state-of-the-art everything. They are so busy paying the bills that they don't get to create much. At the same time, I have friends filming with a Bolex, doing cuts only edits on VHS machinery, assembling an edit list in a notebook, and begging and borrowing the couple of thousand dollars they spend in electronic post to finish up, who live the creative film maker's life joyously, passionately, and constantly. Finally, your pay check will catch up with your effort as long as you're producing—and if it doesn't, well, some people would rather play the creative game three hundred days a year every year for one hundred years and die absolutely happy.

I have to admit to becoming a real techno-buff. The toys and games possible in electronic post are just amazing. I'm positive that I could spend the national budget on stuff and junk to mess with. A company can make a pretty good buck dealing in used equipment bought from guys who keep buying the best and newest. I'm telling you that the guy who is buying a cuts only rig on three-quarter inch to do his own electronic post is just as thrilled as the guy buying a million dollars worth of D2. Make movies.

My wife has been my girl since I was fifteen years old. In some odd way it tells more about me than anything else. I'm pretty sure she has changed in the more than forty years since we met, but I swear, I can't see the alterations. The experience gives me a big advantage over most old men. The need to stray has never been a problem because she is the most beautiful woman in the world. I knew that the moment I first set eyes on her. Sometimes the tilt of her head or the curve of her back can still blind me. I loved her when we married over thirty-five years ago, yet I can't imagine I was wise enough to handle the way I feel about her now. No matter what else has happened in my life, she has been the foundation of my soul—the strength—the love—the passion.

I joke with people that to be a film maker one must have a wife with a steady job. There is much truth in that, but more than a job she must have faith and courage and passion to hold you up when you can't stand on your own. For me she has given more than I can ever repay. My children are a bonus that make a three ring circus out of what could have been a dull, lonely existence. I am blessed with crazy grandchildren, and the pain of watching them struggle to humanhood is both wonderful and frightening. That's why I'm writing this small prayer to you, the new communicators. Don't let them forget what they are and where they came from.

Make sure that you give history a break. Most men never owned or traded slaves. Most Italians wouldn't know a Mafioso from a duck. Most black men will never smoke crack. Most Jews are not rich. Most southern Americans are not racist pigs. Most of us are creatures of great good will with room at our tables for any stranger. The depth of small bytes of information is so profound in the nineties that every little allusion to a fact, no matter how small or insignificant, can be magnified until it becomes a monster.

There is no need in America for walled cities or laws ad nauseam. We have to find a way to limit the power profit has on the nature of all media. The constant repetition of silliness lends strength to nonsense ideas and events. I see old people living in fear because they are assured by the things they see and hear about current events that the dragon is in the street. I see states building great prisons and destroying their own tax base to house the victims of idiot crimes. I see school systems failing to understand the difference between a boy scout and his pocketknife and a thug.

My girl and I have lived all over this nation. We have lived on both sides of all the tracks everywhere we lived. We have known the rich and famous and the down and out. We have learned that the fear that surrounds us is an illusion of truth. It's a magnification of nonsense and a distortion of reason. Understand the power you have to spread anxiety from pillar to post—make movies.

ABOUT THE AUTHOR

Mike Hirsch, the cowboy—philosopher—freedom fighter—old fat guy—American, lives in Indiana with his girl. He continues to help young communicators by writing his monthly blurb, Ya Wanna Make a Movie?, which appears in *In-Sync Publications*. He is currently working on his second book, but secretly wishes to become king of a wild horse herd.

WHAT PEOPLE ARE SAYING

"I want to express my gratitude to you for the effort you take to write your blurb in *In-Sync* Magazine... Your words are inspiring..."

William Alder
Colorado

"I was impressed by your articles...(and) struck by their humanity. I look forward to each issue (of *In-Sync*)...for the thoughtful insights..."

David Kalat
Virginia

"You've captured the essence of the Stereotyping Sin and its Consequences... You see deception—you tell it like it is. Please. More."

Emilia Scanlan
California

"The common sense philosophies...should be part and parcel of every young person's plan for success in any field..."

Karl Hardman
Pennsylvania

"I found your page in (*In-Sync*) quite a delightful piece of personal philosophy."

Bobby Kenyon
Connecticut

"I was greatly moved by the simple honesty contained in your ad in the February edition of *In-Sync*."

M. C.
California

"Bless your heart for the air of happy freedom your life expresses..."

T. H.
Idaho

"Thank you for your <u>Ya Wanna Make A Movie?</u> page in the *In-Sync* paper. The insights and experiences you share, as well as the glimpses into the past, are truly wonderful!"

M. M.
Florida

"I appreciate your verbal kick in the pants."

D. M.
California

"Keep the good *In-Sync* columns coming!"

J. C.
Tennessee

"Since first seeing your "cowboy" ad in *In-Sync*...I'm a fan."

H. K.
California

"Your words will touch the hearts of many readers. I hope they will join you in making life better for other people."

C. B.
Pennsylvania

"Your philosophy needs to be heard more often..."

M. F.
Indiana

"The content and point of view of your comments are thought provoking. What fun to have one's mind awakened by something interesting and unexpected!"

J. F.
Virginia

"Enjoy your column and read it every month... I don't agree with everything you say...but that's the way it's supposed to be..."

B. W.
Washington

ORDERING INFORMATION

I GOT THIS OLD IN AN HOUR
An Anthology For Living At 24 Frames Per Second

Single copy price . . . $22.45 (Includes shipping and handling)
Indiana residents add 5% sales tax

Send check or money order to:

Katydid Publishing
P.O. Box 2247
Muncie, IN 47307

Or if you prefer:

Phone: (765) 282-3159
Fax: (765) 284-0079
E-mail: katydid@mugjoint.com

Bulk discount rates available upon request.

Visit us on the World Wide Web at:
http://www.mugjoint.com/katydid/